Running Your Own
HAIRDRESSING SALON

Running Your Own

HAIRDRESSING SALON

Christine Harvey and Helen Steadman

Kogan Page
WORKING for **YOURSELF** Series

Acknowledgements

The authors would like to thank Jonathan Simons, Jeff Moore, Robert Neill, Brenda Bond, Terry O'Mahoney, Turk Mahmoud and David Joseph for all their help and advice.

Copyright © Christine Harvey and Helen Steadman 1986

All rights reserved

First published in Great Britain in 1986
by Kogan Page Limited
120 Pentonville Road,
London N1 9JN
Reprinted with revisions 1988

British Library Cataloguing in Publication Data
Harvey, Christine
  Running your own hairdressing salon.
  1. Hairdressing
  I. Title II. Steadman, Helen
  646.7'242'068   TT965

ISBN 1-85091-126-6

Printed and bound in Great Britain by
Biddles Ltd, Guildford

Contents

1. **Introduction** — 7
   Your background 7; The drawbacks 9; Checklist: are you cut out to run your own salon? 10; Personal experiences 11

2. **The Structure of the Business** — 14
   Sole trader 14; Partnership 15; Private limited company 16; Co-operative 17; Franchising 17

3. **Finding the Right Premises** — 19
   Location 19; Finding a salon 20; Viewing 21; A going concern 21; Converting a shop 24; A new unit 26; Renting a chair – a cheap alternative 26; Leasehold or freehold 27; More research 27; Where to live 28; Choosing a name for the salon 29

4. **Raising Capital** — 32
   Calculating the costs 32; Raising the necessary cash 35

5. **Decorating and Equipping the Salon** — 41
   Planning the layout 41; DIY or professional fitting 41; Salon decor 43; Fittings and equipment 47; Ancillary areas 53; The shop-front 54; Music 55; New technology 56

6. **Professional Advice** — 57
   Your accountant 57; Your solicitor 58; Your bank manager 59; The insurance broker 59; Other sources of help and advice 61

7. **Finance and Accounting** — 64
   Working out your prices 64; Keeping the books 65; Banking arrangements 66; Taxation 66; National Insurance 68; Reading your figures and forecasting future trends 69

8. Legal Requirements — 70
Premises 70; Health and safety on the premises 71; Employing staff 73; Responsibilities towards the general public 77; Trading legislation 78

9. Employing Staff — 79
Staff recruitment 79; The interview 83; Contracts of employment 84; Dismissing staff 85; Methods of staff payment 86; Communicating and motivating 87; Employing specialists 89; Rent a chair 90

10. Training — 91
The value of training 91; Initial training 92; Adult training 94; In-salon training 94; Business training 95; Beauticians 96

11. Marketing and Selling — 97
The importance of an image 97; Choosing a logo 99; Checklist of printing requirements 99; Promoting your services 100

12. Buying Stock — 105
Choosing your suppliers 105; Own-brand packaging 107; Methods of payments 107; Stock control and rotation 107; Trade shows and exhibitions 109

13. The Daily Operation of the Business — 111
Communicating with clients 111; Client record cards 114; Appointment books 114; Awareness of client purchasing power 114; In-salon entertainment 114; Dealing with customer complaints 115; Crises 117; Regular salon requirements 118; Controlling salon costs 120; Salon security 120; Safety and first aid 122

14. Forward Planning — 123
Future expansion 123; Anticipating problems 128; Looking to the future: planning for your retirement 129

15. Further Information — 131
Useful addresses 131; For further reading 135

Chapter 1
Introduction

Hairdressing has always been a craft which lends itself very much to the independent, small business. It does not require an enormous financial investment to set up and run your own salon: the essential ingredients for success are first, a high standard of hairdressing, both on the part of the owner/manager and the staff; and second, good management and business skills. It is with the second of these essential qualities that we are mainly concerned in this book. It has often been said in the past that if you were a good hairdresser, the rest would inevitably follow, but in our current tough economic climate, hairdressing skills need to be allied to a keen business sense if you are to achieve what must be your main goal in starting your own business: healthy profits.

Few people get rich working for someone else, especially in hairdressing, where, even though many people are paid more than the Wages Council minimum rates, the best way to make real money is to run your own salon.

There is also the added attraction, in working for yourself, of freedom and independence. This is not, of course, unlimited: you have to satisfy your clients, even the awkward ones, otherwise you will soon be closing your doors; and there is legislation controlling what you can and can't do. Nevertheless, within these limitations, you have considerable freedom to choose where, with whom and how you run your business.

Your background

Most hairdressing salons are run by owner-managers who have spent a few years working for someone else, and have seen the opportunities for branching out on their own. These are the people probably best equipped to deal with the day-to-day problems of running a salon, since they can build on their existing experience, and will have come across many of the problems first-hand.

It is an advantage, but not necessary, to have managed a salon for someone else, before setting up your own. Such experience will have given you greater insight into matters such as dealing with staff, bookkeeping and the control of costs. But it is still quite different when you are the owner, because it is no longer 'just a job'. A manager's salary is paid, come what may; if profits dip, you will be the first to suffer, once you are running your own shop.

People who have been away from hairdressing for some time – married women, for instance, who have been bringing up a family – often want to return to the industry, and, with greater maturity and experience of dealing with all the 'managerial' problems that running a household entails, may be thinking in terms of being their own boss, rather than working for someone else. Married men and women, with working partners, stand a particularly good chance of succeeding, since they are likely to be better established, financially, than younger people, and not totally dependent on the profits of the business for their livelihood. They can therefore plough back more of their profits into the business.

Of course, you don't actually have to be a hairdresser to own and run a hairdressing salon. People who are already in business on their own account in another field are often attracted to salon ownership because hairdressing is a predominantly cash business, without the problems of delayed payment so common in other industries.

As a non-hairdresser investing in a salon, you may choose to run the business yourself, engage a manager, or go into partnership with an experienced stylist. If the scale of your operation is to be fairly small, it is best to run the salon yourself, as a manager's salary would be a substantial drain on profits. However, in a small salon, there isn't sufficient 'management' work to justify your full-time presence on the premises, so you really need to take appropriate training, and be able to carry out at least some hairdressing operations yourself. (Courses for adults who wish to gain the necessary skills are described in Chapter 10.)

Employing a manager means, obviously, that you must find a fully competent person, and it is preferable to arrange some form of profit-sharing or incentive scheme to ensure that the manager is fully motivated. A non-hairdressing owner will, in any case, want to be clued up on all the background information relating to the business, and we hope that this book will serve as a practical guide.

A form of business arrangement that is attractive on many

counts, both to working hairdressers and people from other backgrounds, is a partnership. This can be particularly successful if the skills, or assets, of the partners are complementary: one, for instance, specialising in administration – bookkeeping, reception, 'selling' the salon etc – freeing the other partner to concentrate on developing a really high standard of professional hairdressing. Or a hairdresser might team up with a beautician, to run a hair and beauty salon, or with an Afro stylist, to cater for that special market segment.

The drawbacks

There are considerable advantages in running your own salon, such as independence, job satisfaction, creative freedom, and financial rewards. On the other hand, there are also plenty of drawbacks, and you need to think about whether you can cope with the problems involved.

Unlike a 'job', working for yourself means total responsibility. It is easy, when you are employed by someone else, to go home in the evening and forget about your work. But it is much harder to do this when you are responsible for making all the decisions upon which the success of the business depends.

Because you are wholly responsible for the salon's success, you will need to put in much longer hours than any employee. You will want to be on the premises at the busiest periods – which are generally the times of day when other people are free, that is, lunch-times, evenings and Saturdays. Then when you close the salon, you will have to total up the day's takings, enter them in your books, and take care of any problems that you've put off during the day. All in all, it means that instead of working a 40-hour week, you are more likely to be putting in 50 to 60 hours. This will inevitably have repercussions on your private life.

If you are married, you need the support of your partner in the new venture. Unfortunately, it is still generally accepted that a man can devote all his energies to building up a business, and that his wife will back him to the hilt. But it is much more difficult for a woman (and a high percentage of salon owners are women) to gain the sympathy, understanding and practical help that she needs from her partner if she is to devote her energies to running a business. It is important for the couple to talk this through together, and to come to some sort of arrangement for sharing housework, childcare etc – or to engage paid help. Otherwise, a woman who is trying to be the 'perfect' housewife and salon owner-manager is going to be under a great deal of stress. For general health and peace of mind, you need *some* time every week for relaxation: even if it's only for a few hours. And nowadays, a man setting up a business ought also to talk the pros and cons through with his partner first, and discuss how it will affect their joint lives.

The other major pressure on you, besides time, will involve decision-making and problem-solving. Crises like staff shortages, burst boilers, and power cuts are an inevitable fact of salon life, and you're the one who carries the can – it's up to you to decide what action to take, and to cope with the problems as best you can. If you are a 'worrier' by nature, it might be all too easy to let these problems get on top of you. It is difficult to draw a balance here, because *some* anxiety is a good thing, and can act as a motivator. But too much worry and you'll become a nervous wreck. So you need to be sufficiently easy-going to tolerate uncertainty, but enough of a worrier to get things done: a difficult juggling act.

There is considerable risk involved in any business venture. If things don't work out, you could stand to lose a great deal of money; though of course, you might instead make a killing. However, if you're not prepared to put any savings you have into the business, and possibly to offer your house as security for a business loan, then think again.

Checklist: are you cut out to run your own salon?

Ask yourself the following questions, and be *honest*. After you've thought about the answers, you could ask a close friend to look at the questions as well, and you could compare your answers with your friend's assessment of your character and ability.

Personal qualities

1. Are you self-confident, and prepared to tackle a range of new tasks?
2. Do you have good health and stamina?
3. Are you prepared to work hard, and to put 100 per cent effort into the business?
4. Are you able to keep cool in an emergency?
5. Are you good at dealing with people? Can you put up with them day in, day out? Are you tactful? Are you good with children? Are you a sympathetic listener?

6. Are you able to lead and motivate others?
7. Do you have the support of your husband/wife?

Skills, aptitudes

8. Will the things that you do well at in your present job stand you in good stead once you are running your own business?
9. (If you are a hairdresser) Are you creative? How can you develop your skills, and those of others?
10. To what degree do you possess financial and business acumen? How can you improve, and develop this?
11. Do you handle money carefully? Can you save?
12. Are you willing to take advice from professionals – accountants, solicitors and bank managers?
13. Do you see life as a continual process of learning?
14. Are you willing to take risks?

Resources

15. Have you any savings, to help you to get started?
16. Have you any other assets, such as your own home, or a life insurance policy, which you can use as security for a loan?
17. Will you have any other source of income, such as a husband's or wife's salary, apart from the profits of the business? (This is not absolutely necessary, but is helpful at the beginning.)

If you have answered 'yes' to most of these questions, you are in with a chance. If you are doubtful about more than one or two points, then you should really sit down and think about whether running a business is right for you.

Personal experiences

Much of this book is based on Christine Harvey's personal experience in running her own salon, Through the Looking Glass. She bought it in 1976, with advice and support from her husband Jim, who was already in business on his own account.

With a client base of friends and contacts in the local area (a prosperous London suburb), the salon, which had previously been very run down, soon developed into a thriving business. But Christine, who had previously worked for the Ginger Group in the West End, also managed in the meantime to keep up some freelance work in town, and after five years she decided to open a second salon in Kensington, to cater for her Central London clients. This is now doing so well that she has opened up a third salon in Ealing. She also teaches.

Christine is not, however, a writer; and following her own maxim that if you don't know how to do something, you should use the services of someone who does, the book is a collaborative effort, with the writing, and some of the more general business information, contributed by myself, Helen Steadman, a full-time freelance journalist.

We have also talked to several other successful owner/managers:

Brenda Bond, who runs two salons, Peppermint Green and Peppermint Green Studio. Before setting up on her own, she worked as a technician for Wella, and in the course of her job visited hundreds of different salons. Starting her own was very much a case of 'What they can do, I can do better', as indeed she has. Starting with very little capital, she took over premises which had previously been a boutique, and did the place up on a shoestring, with the help of friends. Her clients are mostly professional people, and she finds that she can charge prices that are 'towards the top end of the range': a policy which has given her a firm profit base on which to expand.

Robert Neill, who trades under his own name, was managing a salon when he was only 19, and has been running his own business since the age of 21. He, too, has recently opened a second salon, where he offers beauty treatments along with the usual hairdressing services.

Robert feels that people who are thinking of starting their own salons should ask themselves whether they can really cope when the going gets tough. 'There's a lot of pressure: from the business side, from staff, from everyone, really. Everything'll be going fine and then a basin might crack, or you've no hot water; you've got to be prepared to take all that.' He thinks, too, that 'Anybody starting up has to be very involved in the salon; you've got to add your personal stamp to it.'

'Turk' Mahmoud and David Joseph, partners in Mane Attraction, both have experience of running their own shops. They joined forces in order to expand, with the partnership providing the opportunity to stay open six days a week, employ more staff, and cater for all types of hairdressing. Their shared overheads mean

that they save on costs, can invest in more stock, and have capital available to develop the business.

Turk and David have only been together for a few months, but are already reaping the benefits of a complete salon refit, which has changed the image of the business, bringing in a younger, more affluent clientele.

Terry O'Mahoney, who owns TJ's, bought out his employer, and has managed to make a modest success of a business in an unpromising location: a large, run-down housing estate. He feels he owes his good fortune to the friendly atmosphere of the salon, and the fact that, unlike the previous owner, he pays his staff well.

'I think you've got to believe in yourself,' Terry comments. 'When I go to a show and see someone styling hair, I want to get up there and do it myself, because I think I can do better. I think you've got to have that confidence.'

Chapter 2
The Structure of the Business

Once you have taken the decision to start up your own hairdressing salon, you should seek advice from your bank manager, solicitor and accountant. But even before this, you will need to consider the format your proposed business will take. You have various options open to you – you can either go it alone, as a sole trader; you team up with a partner or partners; you can set up a limited company; or you can form a co-operative. You may also be interested in the possibility of a franchise agreement, whereby you receive support from a nationally established organisation in return for a set percentage of takings.

Sole trader

Most hairdressers start off as sole traders, and certainly operating on this basis is the least complicated way of running a business, involving a minimum of red tape. A sole trader doesn't necessarily work alone – he or she can employ others – but *is* totally and solely responsible for the business. The main advantage of being a sole trader is that you can take all the profits of the business, after allowing for income tax. You also have the advantage of independence, and there are certain tax benefits (also applicable to partnerships, but not to limited companies) in that it is possible to offset losses in the first years of the business against previous tax paid under PAYE. The principal drawback, however, is that you are personally liable for the debts of the business, and if you go bankrupt, your personal possessions (car, home, even clothes) can be taken and sold in settlement.

Starting up as a sole trader involves few formalities. You do not have to register the business, although you should register for VAT if your turnover is likely to be at or above the VAT limit (for further details, see page 66). You should also inform your local tax inspector of your intention to start up a business. There are, of course, other regulations that you will have to take into account when you take over premises and engage staff, but these do not apply to the formation of the business as such.

Partnership

The legal definition of a business partnership is 'the relationship between persons carrying on a business in common, with a view to profit'. It is an association of two or more people. As with a sole trader, each member of a partnership is personally liable for all the debts of the business – even if they were incurred without the knowledge of one or more of the other partners. So setting up a partnership requires careful thought: you shouldn't enter into this type of business arrangement just for the sake of companionship. A partner should be someone who can contribute something to the business – management skills, for instance, or an established hairdressing clientele – that you yourself lack. One important contribution a partner can make is finance; and a sleeping partner, who does little else apart from putting up some money in return for a share of the eventual profits, is well worth considering. This often happens in the case of a family business, where one member of the family runs the salon with the financial backing of the others.

You could also consider a non-hairdressing partner, who would provide capital and do the administrative work – bookkeeping and reception – leaving you free to get on with cutting and styling hair. A middle-aged married woman, for instance, keen to return to work, might be able to raise sufficient capital to invest in a hairdressing business and to work on this basis.

Another variation is to buy into an existing partnership. Such businesses are frequently advertised in the *Hairdressers' Journal*, or you may hear of an opportunity through your existing contacts.

When you enter into a partnership, it is essential (not in law, but for your own protection) to have a formal partnership agreement drawn up by a solicitor. Even the best of friends, or married couples, can fall out, and there are bound to be disagreements from time to time. So think about the following points:

- How the profits are to be divided.
- How much money each partner can take out of the business.
- Which person is responsible for which aspects of the business.

- How decisions affecting the business are to be taken, eg by vote or delegation of responsibility.
- What happens when a partner wants to withdraw from the business (or dies). How is his or her share of the salon to be divided?
- What disciplinary action do you take when one partner does not pull his or her weight? How can existing partners be got rid of and new ones admitted?

As with sole traders, there are no other formalities to be observed in setting up a partnership, except for VAT registration and informing the local tax inspector.

Private limited company

Operating as a sole trader, or partnership, is fine for most small independent salons. If your plans are more ambitious, however, you might want to consider the possibility of setting up a private limited company (probably not at the outset, but later on, once your business has established itself). The advantage of a limited company is that it has a distinct and separate identity from that of the shareholders who own it, and consequently, if the company goes bankrupt, the claims of the creditors are limited to the assets of the company. However, this benefit is cancelled out if the directors of the company extend their liability by giving personal guarantees to the bank, as security for a business loan, which often happens in the case of new and untried businesses.

Directors of limited companies also lose certain tax advantages, in that they are treated as employees of the business and have to pay tax on PAYE, as well as Class 1 National Insurance (for more on National Insurance, see page 68).

For these reasons, it is generally not worth setting up a limited company if you are starting a small, independent salon. It is always possible to change the legal structure of the business later on, however, if your accountant thinks this is advisable.

Should you wish to form a limited company, you will need appropriate professional help: some solicitors and accountants specialise in registering companies. There are also company registration agents who sell 'ready-made' companies, which is a quicker and cheaper process.

Co-operative

This is a somewhat unconventional choice, but quite feasible if you believe in running the business on democratic lines, and avoiding the 'boss and worker' syndrome.

A co-operative is jointly owned and controlled by its members – who are usually the people who work in it, but can include others such as suppliers, friends or relatives. Profits are shared, and decisions (especially major ones) are made jointly. This creates a much greater sense of involvement on the part of those who work in the business, but it can mean that decision-making is a time-consuming affair. It is, on the whole, not an appropriate form of organisation for a hairdressing salon unless everyone involved in the business is able to take equal responsibility.

For further information on co-operatives, contact the Co-operative Development Agency, 21 Panton Street, London SW1Y 4DR; tel 01-839 2988.

Franchising

Another option which may be of interest is franchising. It is not a form of business structure like the choices outlined above – in theory, a franchise could be operated by any of them. Franchising is, instead, a form of business *arrangement* in which a parent organisation (the franchisor) lays down a blueprint for operating the business, covering the content and nature of the goods or services being offered, price and performance standards, design and layout of premises, training and back-up support. In return, the person operating the franchise (the franchisee) pays an initial fee and a royalty.

Franchising is becoming a popular way of setting up a business, mainly because it is much less risky than other kinds of new business venture. The concept will no doubt be familiar – many well-known high street names, such as Wimpy bars, are operated under franchises.

The advantages of operating a franchise include:

- having a proven business system and formula
- training and back-up support
- management expertise
- national advertising and promotion
- salon layout, decor and design as part of a total 'package'
- assistance in raising finance.

However, there are certain drawbacks, principally that of having less freedom than if you are operating a completely independent business, and also that of having to pay a percentage of your takings to the franchise company.

If you are thinking of taking up a franchise, it is essential that you take professional advice from your accountant and solicitor, to determine whether the franchise is financially viable and that the terms are fair. It is also a good idea to talk to other people who have taken up the same franchise, to see what their experience has been, and to check whether the franchisor is a member of the British Franchise Association (though there may be good new franchises that haven't been established for long enough to qualify for membership).

A company offering franchises in the hairdressing business is: Command Performance International Ltd, High End, Troutstream Way, Loudwater, Herts WD3 4LQ; tel 0923 777636.

Whatever form of business structure you choose, remember that you can change, later on, if appropriate. For instance, Turk Mahmoud, after running his own shop on a sole trader basis, decided to go into partnership with David Joseph in order to expand the business. The choice of business structure is not a once-and-for-all decision.

Chapter 3
Finding the Right Premises

Location

Location is a key factor in the success of any type of business which sells to the general public, including, of course, a hairdressing salon.

As a novice owner, you probably won't be able to afford a prime location in a city centre, close to the 'crowd pullers' such as Marks and Spencer, or Woolworths. The chances are that you will have to settle for something more modest – a surburban shopping centre, or a salon in a side-street, for instance – and hope that your own skill and reputation will compensate for whatever the location lacks in potential passing trade.

However, even two salons which appear, at first glance, to be in similar locations – let's say in a small parade of shops in a suburban street – may be surrounded by very different 'catchment areas' (that is, the people who live nearby, who are your potential customers). The first district may be composed mainly of elderly people, who would visit the 'shampoo and set' type of salon but wouldn't have any use for 'cut and blow dry'. The second, on the other hand, could be an up-and-coming area with young professionals moving in – with great potential for the more up-market, fashionable salon.

This is why, when you're looking for premises, you shouldn't simply go for the cheapest place you can find, or the one that is nearest to your home, or is attractively decorated. First and foremost you should investigate the *market* for your services. The salon decor can always be changed, you can always travel a little further to work, and a more expensive rent may be justified by higher turnover. What you cannot change, however, is the potential of the surrounding district. You might, for instance, dream of running a salon in a quiet country village – but if the population only amounts to two or three hundred, there just won't be sufficient demand for your skills to keep you in business.

Numbers aren't the only factor – the type of hairdressing that people require is also important. Do they want mostly blow-dries? Can they afford the more expensive services, such as perming or colouring, that are more profitable from your point of view? Is there a market for specialist work, such as beauty treatments?

It will all depend very much on the local people. If, for instance, you are starting up in a depressed area with high unemployment, you won't be able to charge high prices – but if you can offer a good basic service, people will come to you. If you are in a coastal resort with an ageing population, then a lot of your regular trade will be shampoos and sets, though there may be a seasonal factor, with extra business generated by summer-time holidaymakers.

You can get some idea of the type of trade that does well in a particular locality by checking out the other salons in the area. Go and have your hair done at a few of them (or ask your friends to) – not to 'spy', but to see what sort of clientele they attract.

You can also get a fairly accurate impression of an area by 'pounding the pavement' – walking around and sensing the local atmosphere. In a car, you don't get much idea, because everything passes too quickly. Get out your walking shoes and really observe what's going on – how well the local shops are doing, whether the people are well-dressed, whether it is an area in which you feel comfortable.

Finding a salon

It is probably most sensible to choose the area in which you are going to start your business, and then look around for suitable premises, but if you do it the other way round – choosing the salon first – then do make sure you consider the potential of the local area, as we've described.

There are various ways of finding suitable premises:

- Through high street estate agents, who usually handle commercial as well as residential property;
- Through commercial property agents;
- Through business transfer agents, who specialise in selling existing businesses;
- By looking at advertisements in other publications: *Dalton's Weekly* carries quite a number of advertisements for hairdressing salons; and the *Hairdressers' Journal* has a regular 'Business for Sale' column.

Before you can actually go and view any properties, you need to have a rough idea of what you can afford. You are advised to read Chapter 4 which covers the question of raising finance in some detail, and then to approach your bank manager or accountant for a preliminary discussion, which will give you some indication of the amount you will be able to raise. With a price range in mind, you can then go and view suitable properties.

Viewing

It is advisable to go and view as many properties as you can. The first one you see may seem to be exactly what you want; but it is likely that, as with buying a house, you learn what to look for through practice over a period of time.

It will help you to draw up a checklist of property requirements, so that you have a clear idea of what you are looking for, and a means of comparing different properties at a glance. A suggested format for the checklist is given on page 22.

There are several types of premises you might consider:

A going concern

A going concern is a hairdressing salon that is already in business. You take it over lock, stock and barrel – including the existing stock, fixtures and fittings; and you normally continue to employ the staff who have been working there.

- The business is ready for trading from day 1. You don't need to do anything except go in and open up the shop; you can be taking money as soon as the salon is yours.

- You will be able to make an accurate forecast of running costs (rent, rates, insurance, fuel bills etc) from the previous owner's accounts.

- You will also be able to predict likely takings – although don't rely too much on the accounts that you are shown, and don't be too certain that the existing pattern of business will repeat itself.

- The salon is likely to have an established clientele (again, don't count on this – the previous owner may be selling because trade is slack, or may be planning to take clients with him or her to a new salon).

	Ideal	Property A	Property B	Property C etc
Location				
Parking				
Public transport				
Size (in sq ft)				
Layout				
Plumbing				
Heating				
Lighting				
Ventilation				
Flooring				
Fixtures and fittings (in the case of a going concern):				
– styling units				
– basins				
– chairs				
– dryers				
– laundry facilities				
When available?				
Costs:				
– purchase				
– lease: lease premium rent review				
– rates				
– legal costs				
– moving in costs and support heating/lighting/ plumbing/ ventilation/ decoration				
Constraints:				
– planning permission				
– refurbishing				
– restrictive covenants				
– future expansion				
– neighbours				

On the whole, taking over an existing salon offers the best chance of success, with the minimum of risk. There are, however, a number of points you need to take into account when negotiating with the previous owner:

1. You must examine the audited accounts of the business for the previous three years. You can rely on the overheads of the business being accurately recorded, because they are deductible for tax purposes. You can therefore copy the figures for rent, rates, lighting and heating, and use them when you are drawing up your proposal for the bank. You can also take the owner's figures for stock purchases as being accurate, because again these outgoings can be offset against tax. The amount of money spent on stock will give you some indication of the type of trade the salon has been doing – if the turnover is high, but little has been spent on stock, it could mean that the salon has been mainly providing inexpensive services, and so perhaps there might be potential for boosting trade by doing more perms and tints. On the other hand, a high stock figure coupled with a low stated turnover could mean that the owner has overstated the takings of the business. He or she may claim to have understated the turnover in the audited accounts for tax purposes, but you must ignore this, and base your calculations only on the audited figures, because these are the only ones the bank will consider when you apply for a loan.

2. Look at the appointments book. This, again, may not be accurate, but you can get at least some inkling of the true extent of business by comparing the information about past appointments (particularly for perms and tints, where stock is used) with the amount of stock that has actually been bought. Then work out an average weekly figure for stock purchases, and for turnover, and compare them with a week's appointments and with the prices the salon is charging. This should tell you a lot about the business, and about whether the owner's figures are accurate. Any discrepancies should at least arouse questions in your mind.

3. If the asking price includes a figure for goodwill (which is common practice), then remember that this is an intangible asset – you might change the name of the salon, the customers and staff might not stay. Make sure that only a small percentage of what you are charged is classified under the heading of goodwill.

4. The value of the fixtures and fittings is difficult to calculate, unless they are relatively new. Their real value is their use in helping you to earn profits from the business. But if you plan to strip them out and refit the shop, their value to you is almost negligible; sold second-hand, they would fetch very little. So if you can't bear to live with the existing fixtures and fittings, consider carefully whether it is still worth taking the salon.

5. If stock at valuation is included in the asking price (as is common practice), you should ask the previous owner to supply you with a stock sheet so that you know exactly what you can expect to find when you take over the salon. The sheet should be signed by both you and the vendor when the property changes hands. (You can, if you wish, engage an independent stocktaker to value the stock and advise on a fair price. Look in the Yellow Pages under 'Stocktaking Services'.)

It may be helpful to visit a going concern first as a customer, before you view it as a potential purchaser. This will give you an accurate impression of how the business functions on a normal working day, when the staff and the owner are not on their best behaviour.

Converting a shop

An alternative to buying or renting a going concern is to take over an empty shop which has previously been used for some other type of business, and to convert it into a hairdressing salon. You will have to obtain planning permission to do so, and when you find a property you should check with your solicitor whether it will be possible to obtain the necessary consents (some shops, for instance, have restrictive covenants which prevent them from being used for certain types of trade). Take into account the fact that it can be time-consuming to obtain planning permission.

Starting from scratch with an empty shop will mean that you have to put in plumbing and electrical wiring, decorate, and install all the necessary fixtures and fittings. This can have certain advantages in that you don't have to put up with equipment and decorations installed by the previous owner that are not to your taste. You can lay out the salon exactly as you wish, and you should be able to design it so that you and your staff can operate at maximum efficiency.

On the other hand, you will have the hassle of co-ordinating all the work carried out by builders, decorators, electricians and plumbers – and while the conversion work is going on you will have to cover overheads, but will not have any income. It is important, therefore, that all the work is carried out as quickly as possible.

A more serious drawback is the lack of an established clientele. You will have to be sure you can attract clients by offering better services or lower prices than the existing salons in the area. Advertising can help – as can special gimmicks such as price promotions – anything to get customers across your threshold. But it will inevitably take time to build up a steady, regular trade.

Personal experience

'I had always said that I wouldn't buy someone else's rubbish,' says Brenda Bond, who converted an empty shop, previously a boutique, into a hairdressing salon. 'Because I couldn't afford very much, the salons on the market in my price range were definitely not doing very well. So I thought the best thing to do was to start from scratch – buy an empty shell, do it up. In my previous job I'd gone into a lot of salons, and seen some very nice ideas that weren't expensive. So I knew it could be done cheaply and tastefully.

'It cost me about £2000 to do it up. The first thing I did was to get the plumbers in, to put in the hot water system. That was essential – I'd been in so many salons where someone turns a tap on and someone else's water goes hot or cold or the pressure goes. So I was determined to get that right.

'My boyfriend and I did most of the decorating, with help from one of the girls I was going to employ, and her boyfriend. We worked day and night, and it took us just 10 days to get it ready for opening.

'I'd definitely decided that we'd open on a Saturday, because if we were going to get any clients at all, we'd get them then. The day before we opened, we worked until about four o'clock in the morning to get the shop ready to open.

'The first day went wonderfully. We just didn't stop. People simply walked in off the street. We were very lucky – considering we had so little money, and we were so green.'

A new unit

A unit in a brand new building, or in premises that have been converted for use as a shop, can have certain attractions. It may be sited in an up-and-coming area, such as a modern shopping centre, and there may be other developments in the pipeline which will increase its trading potential.

The developers of such premises sometimes offer financial incentives – such as an initial rent-free period – to encourage businesses to move in. This would obviously save money during the crucial start-up phase, but on the other hand, you have to weigh this temporary, short-term advantage against the large element of risk involved. There will be no established trade, and it could take a long time to build it up. Also, if the units next to yours are empty when you take over the premises, you might find that they are later occupied by businesses that you definitely don't want as neighbours – such as a fish and chip shop or a pool hall – which, besides creating litter and nuisance, would lower the tone and change the atmosphere of the area.

So do bear in mind that taking property of this kind is something of a gamble.

Renting a chair – a cheap alternative

If, after assessing your resources and investigating the local property market, you decide you can't afford to set up your own salon, you might consider an arrangement whereby you rent a chair or work-space from an established hairdresser, or from someone in a different but complementary field, such as a beautician. You would be self-employed and have the benefits of working for yourself, without all the pitfalls and risks. It would be a half-way house between working for someone else and establishing your own salon later on in your career – giving you valuable experience in the meantime.

Leasehold or freehold

The majority of hairdressing salons are run in leasehold property. The tenant buys a lease for a specified period of years, and then pays an agreed rent for the property during that time.

Before taking on a lease you should examine all the conditions carefully. The rent is likely to be subject to regular reviews, and might double or treble – but you won't suddenly be able to put your prices up to the same extent, so your profit margins will be cut.

You should also examine any restrictive clauses in the lease. It might stipulate that the premises are to be used *only* as a hairdressing salon – so you could be in trouble later if you wanted to diversify into something like beauty treatments. You may not be allowed to sublet, which could restrict your room for manoeuvre. You should also look at your responsibilities for repairs to the building.

Buying a freehold is usually more expensive than taking a lease, but can offer greater financial benefits in the long run. It is more common to find freehold salons which include living accommodation, and if this occupies at least half the building, you may be able to get a building society mortgage on the property.

Borrowing from the building society, if you are able to arrange a mortgage, is the best way of financing the business, since you will be able to repay the money over a longer period of time than in the case of most other types of loan. But it can be difficult to arrange a mortgage on property that is part residential, part business, and you would either have to show that your income from the business would be enough to cover the repayments, or that you have income from another source (such as a husband's salary).

Sometimes lock-up shops (that is, without living accommodation) are sold freehold. These are not a particularly good bet, as in most cases you would be buying half a building, and there could be disputes with the owner of the other half over who is responsible for repairs.

In any event, whether you are taking a lease or buying a freehold, do seek the advice of your solicitor as soon as you have found a suitable property.

More research

Once you have found a place that you are interested in, you need to do some careful research to check that your salon is in the right location to develop into a thriving business. You need to look at the following aspects:

- The flow of people passing by (stand on the pavement and *count* them at different times of day, and on different days of the week).
- Are you convinced that the salon is near the right type of 'catchment area' for a residential or working population?
- How the area is doing generally – whether it is on the way up or down.
- What the competition is – the other salons in the area. (It doesn't necessarily matter if there is another salon very nearby, provided it is catering for a different type of clientele.)
- The availability of public transport – are the major routes close to the salon? This is important from the point of view of attracting the right staff, as well as clients.
- Whether there is adequate parking space nearby.

Do this before committing yourself – and also make sure that your accountant, surveyor and solicitor think that your proposals are sound.

Where to live

Properties with a flat over the shop are generally not worth considering unless you're going to live there yourself, or you want to attract a manager – perhaps someone with London experience, for instance – and you feel that the offer of a job with living accommodation thrown in would be an added incentive.

However, it is possible to let the flat on the open market, and if you wish to do so, information on letting can be obtained from: The Small Landlords Association, 7 Rosedene Avenue, Streatham, London SW16 2LS; tel 01-769 5060, and SHAC, 189a Old Brompton Road, London SW5 0AN; tel 01-373 7276/7841.

Obviously, if you're selling your own house to finance the business, you need somewhere to live, so it's a good idea to have a flat on the premises. The fact that you may also be able to get a building society mortgage on the property is an added incentive.

There are certain advantages in 'living over the shop': you are on hand while any conversion work is carried out initially, and you are there to cope with emergencies as they occur. You also save on travelling costs and, perhaps more importantly, on travelling time.

The main drawback to such an arrangement is that you are always on call – you can never forget about the business on your days off. Inevitably, if you are around, your staff will come to you with problems they can't cope with – and they may expect you to deal with visitors, such as sales reps. However, at least you won't have to travel in for miles if there is a crisis.

If you are not planning to live on the premises, try to avoid taking a shop too far from where you live. By the time you've worked a late night, and done the books, the last thing you want is an hour's journey home; you are only adding unnecessarily to the stresses and strains of running the business.

Choosing a name for the salon

Choosing a name for the salon requires careful thought, because it sets the whole image of your business, and indicates the type of clientele you are aiming at.

You may already have a fairly clear idea of the type of salon you want to run, so choose a name that is in keeping with your image. Ideally, the name should be short, to the point, and timeless (you don't want to have to change it two or three years later). It must give an impression of the type of service you are offering, and it must be something that sticks in the mind – a name that's catchy enough for the clients to remember. Bear in mind that your employees and clients have to be able to pronounce it easily – it has to roll off the tongue when you or your staff answer the phone.

To set you thinking

A straightforward choice is simply to use your own name – Hair by Barbara – for instance. Or if the salon is a partnership, you could combine the two names – Philipsharon (the proprietors being Philip and Sharon) – is short and catchy.

Some people choose a name that shows they have London or big-city experience – Ronald of Bond Street, for example. Others find that their surname is well known because it has associations with other products – Benson, for instance is widely publicised by Benson & Hedges – so it might stick in the mind.

Initials, like first names, are catchy and won't date. Maurice John Miller, for instance, has called his salon MJM. Another simple variation is to use your street number – if you're at 53 Waldorf Road, then why not call yourself Salon 53? Or at number one, you could use the name Salon One.

Names that are puns, such as Curl up and Dye, are great fun. Names which reflect hairdressing terms – Croppers, Rough Cut – are popular at the moment.

Foreign names, because of the potential pronunciation problems, can cause difficulties – although if you are aiming at a particular group of people who will be familiar with the name, then by all means go ahead.

Specialisations
If you're specialising, you'll want this to be reflected in the name of your business. If you offer beauty treatments, show it in the name you choose – a name like Emma Clare: Health, Hair and Beauty says it all. Afro stylists will obviously want their name to indicate what they do – Black Beauty is an excellent example. If you're planning to sell hair products, then a name like The Hair Shop would convey the right information.

You may want to incorporate the word 'unisex' into the name, or to display it prominently on your shop-front. If you don't like the term, then 'hairdressing for men and women' conveys the same message.

If you're a men's hairdresser, then of course you will want a fairly butch, macho sort of name.

Don't clash with the competition
Do check that the name you have chosen, or a similar name, is not being used elsewhere in the area. Christine considered the name Harvey's until she found out that a nearby salon was called Halver's. As well as causing confusion, a clash like this means that your hard work goes towards building up someone else's reputation.

The Yellow Pages will list the names of your local competitors.

Changing the name
If you buy an existing salon, you may wish to continue trading under its previous name. But do check on the reputation it has established – if it hasn't been successful, you would be well advised to use a new name to indicate the change of ownership.

Rules and regulations
If you are a sole trader or partnership, trading under your own surname(s) (with or without first names or initials) then no further formalities are needed. This is also the case of limited companies using their full corporate names.

However, if you intend to trade under another name (calling your salon Hairstyle, for example) then you have to disclose the name and business address of the owner(s) (or directors of a limited company) on all business letters, written orders for the supply of goods or services, invoices and receipts, statements and demands for payment of business debts. Limited companies also have to show their registration number and the address of their registered office. Additionally, you have to display this information prominently in your business premises.

There are certain names whose use is restricted: these include names which imply national or international pre-eminence (such as International, British or English) or which imply business pre-eminence or representative status (Federation, Institute). Special permission has to be obtained for the use of such names.

Further information can be obtained from the Companies Registration Office, or from the Small Firms Service.

Chapter 4
Raising Capital

If you are lucky, and find the right premises, you may not need a great deal of capital to start a hairdressing business. But you will certainly need *some* money, and although you will probably have to use your own savings, you may also be obliged to borrow from outside sources.

In any case, you need to know, first of all, exactly how much it is going to cost to set up the business, and second, how much the running costs are going to be. You need this information in order to arrive at a sensible pricing policy – it is no good having a hundred customers every week, each paying an average of £9, if you need £800 just to keep the business ticking over – you would be left with only £100 profit for your pains. You also need the information in order to present a reasonable case to the bank manager, or other money-lender.

Calculating the costs

The costs of starting the business

First you have to calculate the amount you need to spend on a once-and-for-all basis, just to get the business off the ground. You will need to take into account the following costs:

- The initial premium on premises, if you are renting; or if you are buying on a mortgage, the deposit.
- Purchase of equipment. It may save you much-needed cash to lease large items, such as a dryer bank or steamer, or to buy them on hire purchase. But there will in any case be small items – brushes, combs, rollers and so forth – that have to be bought.*

---

*You can save some money, at the outset, if you register for VAT *before* you buy any equipment. In this way, you can reclaim VAT on your purchases. If you postpone registration, you will not be entitled to a refund. Further information on VAT is given on page 66.

- Stock – including shampoos, tints, perming lotion etc. Don't overstock; you don't want your capital to be tied up in unsold items. Operate with a limited range, and replace quick-selling lines later on.
- Refitting and decorating the premises. This is important, because the salon's decor sets the tone and image of the business. But if you are starting on a shoestring, you may be able to do some of the work yourself – or perhaps friends or relatives could help out.
- Installation of phone, and any other necessary services.
- Legal and other professional fees.
- Stationery – appointment cards, letterheads etc, printed with the name of the business.

Working capital

Although hairdressing is a cash business – that is, the customers pay you immediately for your services – you will still need some money, in addition to the start-up costs, to tide you over the first few months while the business is establishing itself. If you are setting up a brand new salon, for instance, your takings in the first month are probably not going to be enough to cover all your running costs. So you need to allow some extra margin – which is known as 'working capital' – to get you through this early period.

Running costs

Having worked out how much it will cost just to start the business, you then need to calculate how much it will cost to keep it going. Running costs (or overheads) will include:

- Rent (or mortgage repayments)
- Rates (general and water rates)
- Insurance
- Fuel bills
- Telephone
- Staff wages (remember to include cleaners and casual labour)
- Repairs, depreciation on equipment
- Cleaning
- Laundry
- Interest on loans and hire purchase, bank charges
- Fees for professional services (accountant, solicitor)
- Trade subscriptions
- Staff refreshments

- Periodicals and magazines
- Your own travelling expenses
- Advertising
- Printing, postage and stationery.

Having added up the running costs of the business, and taken into account the regular payments on any loans negotiated to cover the cost of your mortgage or your lease and the costs of starting your business, you can then calculate a 'break-even' point. This is the amount you need to take each week (or month, or year, depending on the period you've chosen) just to pay the bills – before you make any profit. Say, for example, you work out that on a weekly basis, you will reach your break-even point if your takings are £1000. Above this figure, anything that comes in is profit. So if, for instance, you want to make a profit of £400 per week, then your takings will have to be £1400.

Of course, one vital item that we haven't yet considered is your personal budget – the money you need to take out of the business to cover your own living expenses. If you are running the business on a sole trader or partnership basis, then you pay income tax on the profits, just as if they were your 'salary'. You also have to pay your own National Insurance contributions, as a self-employed person. So that £400 'profit' will not go straight into your own pocket – you need to leave a reasonable amount to cover tax, National Insurance and any unforeseen expenses. (It is worth considering a separate savings account earmarked solely for tax.)

If, on the other hand, you are running the business as a limited company, you are treated as an employee and must pay tax through PAYE, together with Class 1 National Insurance contributions (both as an employer and employee). Of course, in these circumstances you would still have to take into account your own salary, and that of any other director(s) of the company, before calculating the break-even point.

Prices

Once you know the break-even point, you can begin to work out how much you will have to charge – and how many customers you need to attract – before you can make a profit. Returning to our break-even figure of £1000, that could be reached by having 50 customers, each paying £20, or 100 customers paying an average of £10 – it depends, of course, on the type of market you are aiming for. Don't be too optimistic in your calculations; you need to consider 'idle time', those periods in the day when the salon is quiet. You'll also have to allow for some seasonal variations – your busy period is likely to be just before Christmas, whereas the summer months, when people go away on holiday, may be relatively slack. For more information on pricing, see Chapter 7.

Raising the necessary cash

Having worked out how much it is going to cost you to start the business, you then need to consider how you are going to raise the money. You will probably want to go for a mixture of funds – some of your own money, possibly some from a relative, a loan or overdraft from the bank, or a building society mortgage.

The sources you might consider include:

Your own money

Although you may not have very much in the way of savings, you may be better off than you realise. Your main asset is likely to be your home, if you own it. You could take out a second mortgage, or sell your present home and move to somewhere cheaper (possibly a flat over the salon).

Life insurance or endowment policies are another source of cash, if they have been in force for several years. Most companies will lend quite a high percentage of their surrender value – at interest rates that compare favourably with those of the banks. An alternative is to use the policy as security for a bank loan or overdraft.

Using your own money is the cheapest way of financing the business – interest payments on loans can be 15 per cent a year or more. But if your own resources aren't sufficient, then you will have to look at alternative methods of raising capital.

Money from private sources

A relative or friend of the family may be sufficiently enthusiastic about your proposed salon to consider lending you money at a low or non-existent rate of interest. However, private loans can cause a lot of misunderstanding and heartache if things go wrong. It is important to make sure that the lender understands that he or she is not entitled to a say in the management of the business, and is not a shareholder. A solicitor should draw up a document, setting out the terms of the loan, which should include:

- The rate of interest
- The period over which the loan is to be repaid
- Circumstances in which the loan may be withdrawn.

Rather than lend money directly, a relative or friend might instead be willing to act as a guarantor of your bank overdraft or loan. If you intend to offer this type of personal guarantee as security, then it is advisable to approach that individual's branch bank initially – it is only the manager of that particular branch who is really in a position to assess the value of such a guarantee.

As an alternative to a loan or guarantee, a wealthy friend of the family (but not a relative) can buy a shareholding in your business in a very tax efficient way under the government's Business Expansion Scheme, obtaining up to 60 per cent tax relief on the investment. However, you would have to form a limited company to benefit from the scheme.

Building societies
You may be able to borrow from the building society if you are buying a freehold property which includes living accommodation occupying at least half the building.

You will probably have to pay a rather larger deposit than you would if you were buying wholly residential property, and you may also be asked to pay a slightly higher interest rate, and repay over a shorter term (usually less than 20 years). Nevertheless, if you can arrange such a mortgage, it is a very good way of financing the business.

When you present your case to the building society, you will have to show that the income from the business or from another source (such as your husband's or wife's salary) will be sufficient to meet the mortgage repayments. It will help if you have already had a mortgage on your own home, or have saved with the building society.

Approaching your bank
If you are unable to get a mortgage (for example, if you are not planning to live on the premises) and cannot raise sufficient funds from private sources, your first line of approach should be to one of the high street banks – preferably the one at which you already have an account.

If you are going to borrow from the bank, it is vital that your approach to the bank manager be professional and well thought out. You should prepare a typed *business plan*, which includes:

- Personal information.
- A description of the business, details of the service that you are going to provide, and your market.

- How much money you want, why, how you intend to use it, and how you will repay it; how much you yourself (and your partners or co-directors) can raise.
- If you are taking over a going concern, the audited accounts of the business for the past three years.
- Other financial information. This will include a *budget* and a *cash flow forecast*, which should be prepared on a monthly basis for the first 12 months of operation, and on a quarterly basis for a further two years. A *budget*, which estimates projected sales compared with costs, shows the profitability of the business; it is this that helps to demonstrate the viability of your proposal. A *cash flow forecast* differs from a budget in that it shows when the money actually comes in and goes out, and the borrowing that will be necessary.

This undoubtedly sounds rather technical, and indeed drawing up a budget and cash flow forecast are complicated tasks, made more difficult by the fact that you are expected to *predict* sales. However, if you are buying an existing salon, the accounts of the business will provide a basis to work on. If, on the other hand, you are starting from scratch, it is undoubtedly much more difficult; but in that case you should have done some market research on which to base your projections.

It is advisable to get some professional help in drawing up a business plan; this can be obtained, free of charge, from Local Enterprise Agencies (see page 63). Advice is also available from the government's Small Firms Service, and from accountants, who will often give a free initial consultation. A further possibility would be to take one of the many courses that are available on setting up a small business. All of them (except for one-day introductory courses) will help you to draw up a business plan, as well as guiding you through all the other problems you are likely to encounter in setting up your salon.

How much can you borrow?
As a rule of thumb, the bank manager will expect you to put the same amount of money into the business as the bank does. This 'fifty-fifty' rule is flexible; if your business plan is well thought out, the bank may advance a greater proportion of the necessary funds; but it holds true as a general guideline.

There are two types of bank finance that are relevant to the small hairdressing business, just starting up:

1. An overdraft

An overdraft, which is the commonest form of borrowing for the very small business, has an advantage over other forms of bank lending in that interest is paid only on the amount outstanding. This means that if, as is likely, your receipts – and therefore the amount you need to borrow – fluctuate, it can be a relatively cheap form of finance.

Theoretically, however, an overdraft can be called in at any time. It should, therefore, be used as working capital, rather than to purchase equipment, or to pay for the premium on your premises.

2. A term loan

To pay your premium, or to buy equipment, you may be able to negotiate a short-term loan (for up to three years). It is less likely that the proprietor of a totally new business would be able to get a medium- or long-term loan (for three to ten years or 10 to 20 respectively) but these are obviously worth considering later on, when the business is established.

Security

A common misapprehension is that if you offer sufficient security, you will automatically be able to borrow from the bank. This is not the case – banks are in no way pawnbrokers – and the bank manager will decide to lend you money if he thinks your business proposition is sound, almost irrespective of whether security is offered.

However, if your case, like most business proposals, falls into the 'grey area' between being a sure-fire winner and a guaranteed failure, then security may be helpful, and might tip the balance in your favour.

Assets that may be offered as security include your house or life insurance policy. As we have already mentioned, it may also be possible for a relative or close friend to offer a personal guarantee.

Shopping around

If you don't succeed with your first approach to a bank, don't give up; it is worth shopping around for a loan or overdraft, because each branch manager has considerable autonomy, and going to another bank, or even another branch of the same bank, may pay off.

Finance houses

Sometimes finance houses are recommended as an alternative source of funding. Many finance houses are owned by banks, and the banks may recommend them in certain cases; if you go to any of the others, do check the interest rates charged, as these can be very much higher than rates charged by high street banks.

Government and local authority assistance

A government-run scheme that is of considerable help to people starting new businesses is the Enterprise Allowance Scheme, whereby you can receive an allowance of £40 a week for up to a year in addition to any money earned from the business. There are two catches: one is that you must be unemployed, and receiving unemployment and/or supplementary benefit, at the time of applying for the allowance; and the second is the fact that you must also be starting a new business, not taking over a going concern.

You must satisfy the following conditions to qualify for the scheme:

- You must have been out of work (and receiving unemployment/supplementary benefit), or under notice of redundancy, for at least eight weeks before your application.
- You must be starting a new, small business (not taking over an existing one).
- You should have at least £1000 available which you intend to invest in the business over the first 12 months (this can be in the form of a bank loan or overdraft).
- You have to be over 18 and under 65.
- You must have no other employment while you are receiving the allowance, and you must be prepared to work full-time (at least 36 hours a week) in the business.

If you think you might be eligible for the scheme, ask at the Jobcentre for further details.

Other forms of help depend very much on the area in which you are starting up the business; special loan and grant schemes tend to be targeted on the depressed areas of the country.

Many local authorities run industrial development offices, or their own small business information and advice centres; these are the best source of information about the help that is available locally.

Your search for financial backing
As you can see, there are numerous sources of finance for the small business; but you do have to be well-prepared, and able to present a carefully thought out plan, before you approach a potential lender.

Chapter 5
Decorating and Equipping the Salon

If you are starting from scratch with a new unit, or converting premises that previously served some other trade, you have the advantage of being able to fit out the salon exactly the way you want it. If, on the other hand, you are taking over a going concern, you may want to refit the salon. This creates interest, and demonstrates that the business has a new image. If you can't afford a complete refit, then try some small, inexpensive innovations, just to show the change of ownership.

Planning the layout

You should start off by making a plan on squared paper. In the salon itself, you need to decide on the layout of working positions, basins and dryers. Then you need to map out reception, the coat cupboard, sales display area, tinting and perming section and ancillary areas such as stock room and dispensary, staff room, WCs and laundry.

Your layout will normally be determined by the existing plumbing, unless you can afford to change this. It also depends on the shape of your salon, and the amount of floor space. Generally, one can have four working positions for each 100 square feet of floor space. This takes into account a 'circulation area' – you have to allow not only for the actual space taken up by a styling unit and a chair, but also leave room for staff and clients to walk around without the salon seeming cramped and cluttered.

DIY or professional fitting

It's obviously cheaper to do as much of the decorating and fitting as you can. However, you will end up with a more professional 'look' if you go to one of the specialist companies which provide salon fittings. You can get a good idea of the styles they are currently promoting by visiting the big annual trade fairs.

Running Your Own Hairdressing Salon

THROUGH THE LOOKING GLASS   SCALE 1:20
KENSINGTON SHOP SUGGESTED PLAN

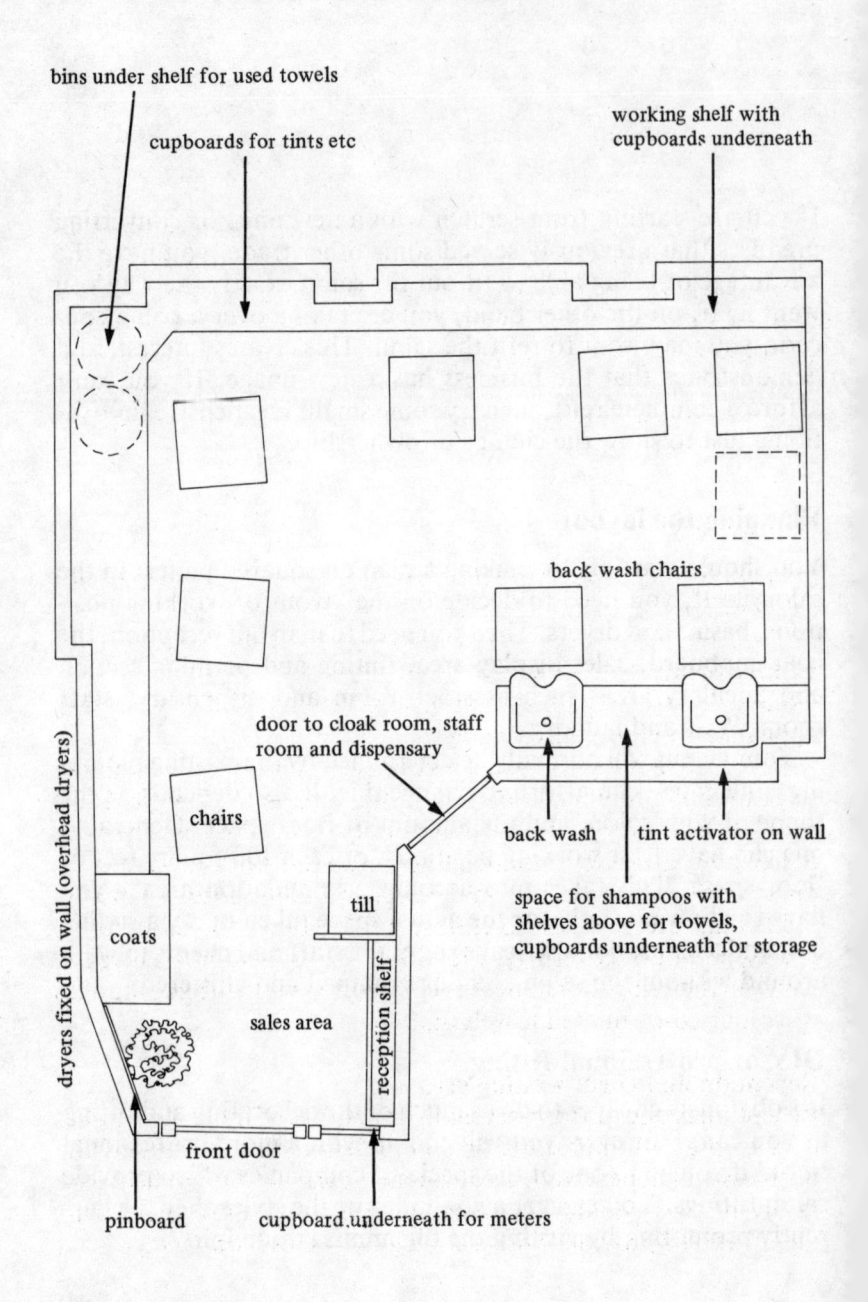

bins under shelf for used towels

cupboards for tints etc

working shelf with cupboards underneath

back wash chairs

door to cloak room, staff room and dispensary

back wash

tint activator on wall

space for shampoos with shelves above for towels, cupboards underneath for storage

dryers fixed on wall (overhead dryers)

chairs

coats

till

reception shelf

sales area

front door

pinboard

cupboard underneath for meters

42

A point that is not always appreciated by new salon owners, who are short of cash and in a hurry to open up the business as quickly as possible, is that you don't have to buy the *full* professional fitting service. If money is no problem, the specialists can arrange everything, including plumbing and wiring. But you can, if you wish, simply commission a design, or design and fitting, but arrange to do the plumbing, electrical work and so on yourself. You can also buy equipment 'off the peg' and fit it yourself.

If you are short of cash, you might also consider hire purchase or leasing arrangements when you are fitting out your salon. One company that offers hire purchase on large items of salon equipment, such as styling units, chairs and reception desks, is Salon Services. Customers pay a fixed deposit of about 25 per cent of the total price, and pay the remainder over two to three years. The company also offers leasing arrangements. Another company, Ogee, has its own finance company, which can offer hire-purchase facilities.

Salon decor

You need to consider, in some detail, the following aspects of salon decor and equipment:

Colour theme
Colour is extremely important in setting mood and tone, and in appealing to your chosen market.

If you are aiming to attract a youngish clientele, it is tempting to go for bold, bright colours, which have a dramatic impact. The problem is, however, that strong colours tend to become difficult to live with after a few months. Pastels, on the other hand – greys, pinks or blues – are easier on the eye, and don't date so quickly.

Playing safe, it's best to choose neutral tones for salon units, chairs, and floor coverings, which will last for a number of years. You can then ring the changes every so often with different ranges of colour co-ordinated towels and gowns.

Reception and client waiting area
Reception is one of the most significant areas of the salon, in that it gives that all-important first impression. The success of the business will depend to a great extent on the way your clients are received: they should be greeted with a smile, have their coats taken, and be provided with a clean gown. This is the first point at

Running Your Own Hairdressing Salon

Professional salon design produced by Renbow, to the customer's specifications

Decorating and Equipping the Salon

which anyone in the salon has physical contact with the client, and the impression given can have a lasting effect.

If space and finance permit, you could have a separate, screened-off reception area, staffed by a full-time receptionist. Of course, there must be sufficient business to justify employing a receptionist – apart from the financial loss, there's nothing worse than looking into a salon and seeing the receptionist knitting, or filing her nails. She should constantly be busy answering the phone, taking money, booking appointments and doing the daily accounts. So if you're just starting up, it's likely that you won't need a receptionist, and in this case, as you, your stylists and juniors will welcome clients, it is more convenient to have a reception area which is not physically separated from the main body of the salon.

Your reception desk will need to be equipped with a till (that can only be opened by the staff), an appointment book, appointment cards, and telephones. You might also want to have music system controls, a computer terminal, and a video screen for client information and sales. Remember that these will need power points.

The client waiting areas should be equipped with comfortable chairs and a rack or table for magazines – the whole aim being to make waiting (which should in any case be kept to a minimum) as pleasant as possible. Reception is an excellent place for a sales display – perhaps a partition with glass at eye level, to display products that clients can look at and touch while they are waiting for their appointments. Product leaflets, produced by the manufacturers, should be freely available. And you may wish to display your price-list on or behind the reception desk (though some people prefer to put it in the window – it's a matter of taste, and of catering to the right market).

You will need a place to hang clients' coats. The position of the coat cupboard is a matter of convenience; if there isn't room at the front of the salon, it *can* be situated at the back, but if you have a long, narrow room, people traipsing backwards and forwards to fetch coats could be a nuisance. On the other hand, if your clients are likely to have expensive coats, an open cupboard at the front could be a temptation to thieves; it is not unknown for a casual passer-by to slip in, unnoticed by the staff, and disappear with a valuable fur coat.

While you can take no responsibility for the security of clients' property on your premises, and you may wish to display a disclaiming notice to this effect, a modicum of security must be offered.

It is bad for customer relations if a client's property goes missing. You might want to introduce a system of cloakroom tickets for clients' coats and shopping.

Fittings and equipment

You will need the following:

Styling units (dressing-out tables)
The type of styling unit you choose will depend both upon the shape of your premises and, of course, on your budget.

At its very simplest, a unit can consist of a shelf and mirror fixed to the wall, designed by you and assembled by a local joiner. If you want a more professional look, you can buy complete or part units from the manufacturers, off the peg (these include footrests, backing boards, shelves, mirrors, canopies, and light-concealing units) or you can order them in conjunction with an overall design plan specially tailored by the manufacturers to your specifications.

If you have a long, narrow salon, you would probably want to have either:

(a) a bank of styling units (which would mean that you'd have no need to decorate between each one); or
(b) staggered units.

With a square room, or an oblong with plenty of space in the middle, you can maximise the number of working positions by using freestanding 'island' units, which are usually double-sided but can include as many as five styling units.

You will need to make sure that you have enough power points near each styling unit, and that they are easily accessible. Shelves need to be wide enough to take hairdryers, setting lotions etc, and possibly to display retail items. Towels must be readily to hand. And if you are planning any overhead or wall-mounted equipment, check with your surveyor that the walls are sound enough to take it.

Basins
Most common nowadays is the backwash, which offers a more modern approach to hair washing than the front wash, where the client leans forward.

As with styling units, it is possible to buy part of a unit (the basin alone) or, a full unit with a base. More sophisticated equipment includes built-in chairs, or backwashes with an adjusting swivel mechanism which adds to client comfort.

A wide range of colours is available, but it might be more practical to go for a fairly neutral colour if you anticipate changing your decor later on; backwashes are expensive to replace, and it would be cheaper to keep the existing ones while changing the colour of the other fittings and the walls.

Near the backwash areas you need easily accessible space for shampoos and conditioners, as well as somewhere to store clean towels.

Chairs
You need various types of chair for different purposes:

- for the backwashes (adjustable chairs are more comfortable for clients);
- for working positions;
- to fit under dryers (these can be bought in the form of a bank of chairs, if required);
- for the reception area;
- for the staff room;
- for specialist beauty treatments. For instance, for facial treatments such as eyebrow shaping, you need a chair that will tilt back; for manicures you need a manicure stool, and for leg waxes or electrolysis, a 'beauty bed'.

The comfort of your clients is obviously a major consideration in choosing chairs. Remember that a client may be spending up to three hours sitting in one of your chairs, so test them out, before you purchase, with this in mind.

Chair covers should be washable – someone's bound to spill perming or tinting solution on them at some stage. It is also worth thinking about whether it will be feasible to re-upholster or re-cover the chairs, should you want to change the salon decor in the future.

You can spend anything from £50, for a basic chair for a working position, to over £1000 for a hydraulic fully adjustable barber-style model, and you have the choice of buying from a specialist supplier or from an ordinary commercial outlet, such as Habitat. You might, for instance, want to go to a specialist for the chairs you are going to use in the salon itself, buy comfortable chairs for reception at a furniture shop, and purchase the staff room chairs second-hand.

Mirrors

There are endless possibilities for using mirrors to make the salon look larger, brighter and more attractive. They can create an illusion of space, bring light to dark corners, and provide an eye-catching backdrop for the display area.

Strategically placed, mirrors can help everyone to see what's going on in the salon, and prevent clients in the perming and colouring area from feeling 'cut off'. They can also help you, as the salon owner, to supervise your staff. Be careful, though, if a mirror reflects what's going on in the staff room – you might want to keep an eye on it yourself, but you might not want the clients to be able to!

As far as purchase is concerned, a low-cost option is to buy your mirrors from the local glass merchants, and install them yourself. Be warned, however, by this cautionary tale: one London hairdresser stuck her mirrors up with builders' glue, not realising that the wall she'd fixed them to wasn't completely flat. The result was a distorted image, as in a fairground 'hall of mirrors'.

In any case, mirrors stuck directly to the wall are not easy to clean without wiping the surrounding paintwork at the same time. It's probably better to use frames, or complete wall units, which can be bought in kit form.

If you are using a firm of shopfitters, they will install your mirrors and provide professional advice on their positioning. It's still worthwhile, however, to buy from the local glass merchants – the glass has to be bought somewhere, and why not promote local goodwill?

Hairdryers

You have a choice of various types:

- Hood dryers, which can either be freestanding, or in banks. Either type can have fitted chairs, or be used with chairs of your choice. Freestanding dryers enable your layout to be more flexible, because they can be moved around the salon as you wish or put into storage when they are not needed.

    Two drying methods are used for hood dryers: with the first, a strong draught is created, and without a hairnet, the hair blows around. The second type, which provides a diffused flow of air, doesn't disturb the hair so much, with the result that natural drying, without rollers, can be achieved.

- Infra-red dryers, commonly known as octopus lamps. There are various different types: for example, a solar lamp which speeds up the development of colours.
- Hand-held blow dryers.

Wall photographs
Hairdressing wholesalers provide a good selection of photographs illustrating current styles, which can be framed and wall mounted. Alternatively, you might prefer to use photographs of your own work (*not* snapshots), to demonstrate your expertise. There are photographic seminars available to help you to produce high quality photographs to display in the salon.

Photographs are helpful to give your clients an idea of general trends, which may perhaps spark off the desire for a change of style. With good colour shots, you can also tempt clients into a change of colour.

Whatever you do, don't leave the same photographs there for ever — nothing looks worse than fading photographs of outdated styles.

Lighting
The most important point to remember about salon lighting is that it has to give true colour. You will therefore have to take into account your overall colour scheme — if you're decorating the walls in dark shades, then the lights will have to be brighter to compensate.

Most salons have a combination of strip lights and downlights to provide overall lighting, together with spotlights to enhance specific areas.

Spotlights generate a lot of heat, and can be expensive to run, so don't overdo their use. Their positioning is important: they mustn't shine into the clients' eyes, nor should they cast a shadow when the stylist is standing in the working position.

Strip lights are cheaper to run than spotlights, though they are not always very attractive, and harsh strip lighting can give people an ashen-faced appearance. You may prefer to use downlights for background lighting in the salon, reserving strip lights for the service areas (staff room, dispensary) where the overall effect is unimportant.

If you are setting up the salon on a shoestring, you can buy perfectly adequate lighting from shops such as British Home Stores. In the long run, though, it is better to go for industrial lighting, and to get professional advice: contact the manufacturers who advertise in magazines dealing with interior design (*Interiors*, *Homes and Gardens*) for price-lists and further information.

When fitting lighting, make sure you employ a qualified electrician.

Heating
Quite surprisingly, the majority of hairdressing salons don't have any heating – sufficient warmth is generated by the hairdryers.

If you do want to put in some form of heating system, skirting board heating, run off the hot water boiler, ought to be sufficient. An inexpensive alternative, that doesn't use up too much space, is freestanding heaters that can be put away in the summer months.

Air conditioning
At the same time as you are thinking about heating, it's worth considering whether air conditioning is necessary. If you can afford it, air conditioning is easier to fit right at the start than later on, but it is expensive, and many small hairdressing salons manage without.

Hot water
The electricity and gas boards sometimes have special promotions, so shop around and see what's available. Make sure that the hot water system you choose has sufficient capacity for the volume of water you are using, and allow for future expansion. Approximately 12 gallons of hot water per hour per basin should be available, at a supply temperature of 130 degrees Fahrenheit. This is mixed with cold supply to give an average working temperature of 105 degrees Fahrenheit.

In case of power cuts or problems with your boiler, consider having a back-up system – if your main water heating is from a gas boiler, for instance, being able to switch over to an electric immersion heater means you should never be without hot water.

Regular servicing of the system is vital. Each time the service engineer visits, make an appointment for the next call – that way, servicing becomes a matter of routine.

Floor covering
It is worth buying good quality, hard-wearing floor covering, that can be easily cleaned. It is a false economy to try to scrimp on this: cheaper flooring will not last as long, and will quickly become tatty-looking in the high-wear areas.

Vinyl is a good choice for floors. Tiles are economical for the high-wear areas, but sheet form, with welded joints, is preferable for parts of the salon where water is present. Another popular option is ceramic tiles – the initial outlay is high, but they are long-lasting, very easy to clean, and less likely to be damaged by chemicals. Wood has certain drawbacks as far as upkeep is concerned, but does look attractive, and if you have an existing wood floor you could sand it, stain it or leave it a natural colour, and either coat it with polyurethane varnish or wax polish it. Any broken floorboards or parquet tiles can be replaced by a carpenter.

For reception, you may want a carpet – if so, choose one that can easily be replaced as soon as it shows signs of wear.

Hairdressing equipment

The equipment you choose is very much a matter of personal taste. Technology, and the way it is used, is changing all the time, and so it is impossible to lay down a fixed set of requirements to suit every salon.

However, the following checklist will help you to select the particular pieces of equipment that *you* need. It is most unlikely that you would want to buy all of them; some are essential for every salon, others very much a matter of choice.

Checklist

- Hood hairdryers
- Hand hairdryers
- Octopus lamps
- Steamers
- Activators
- Roller trolleys or baskets
- Rollers, pins and clips
- Permanent wave rollers
- Curling tongs
- Hair clippers
- Hot rollers
- Hot brushes
- Crimping machines
- Tint bowls
- Tint brushes and combs
- Razors
- Towels
- Gowns
- Tin foil dispensers
- Cling film dispensers
- Sterilising unit/autoclave
- Back mirrors
- Computer systems:
    - for colouring and perming
    - for stock control
    - for client records

Initial opening stock – shampoo, conditioners, a range of colouring and perming products, setting lotions and styling mousses, hair lacquers.

It is usual for smaller hairdressing implements such as scissors and combs to be provided by the individual stylist.

Gowns

If you wish to design and make your own gowns, a good fabric to use is polyester cotton. Because the gowns need to fit all shapes and sizes, buy the extra wide size, normally used for making sheets and duvet covers. This material is very easy to care for, being non-crease, non-iron and drip-dry.

Alternatively, there are companies which specialise in making up gowns to your design specifications, or you can buy gowns 'off the peg' from wholesalers. You can also have your company logo printed on to your gowns – besides 'personalising' your service and giving an impression of attention to detail, this is useful for drawing attention to your salon at fashion shows and demonstrations.

Accessories

Plants induce a restful, tranquil atmosphere. Buy or hire them from the local florist, or specialist supplier. Silk flowers are also worth consideration.

Humidifiers help to reduce condensation.

Ionisers, which create static electricity and oxidise some of the nitrogen in the air to create ozone – a purifying and sterilising agent – may help to make salon life more pleasant. You have to choose the right size, depending on the salon area.

Refreshments. You will need to have a means of making tea and coffee for staff and clients. A kettle, a few cups, a jar of instant coffee and a packet of teabags are the minimum; if you have money to spare, you might want a coffee percolator and cups and saucers which match your overall colour scheme, or a coffee dispenser which can be operated by coins or tokens.

Ancillary areas

Laundry
You need to allow space for a washing machine and dryer, if you plan to do laundry on the premises. (See also Chapter 13.)

Stock room and dispensary
The stock room should obviously be easily accessible to staff. It should be out of sight of your clients, however, both for security reasons (fit a lock if you're worried about this) and because it may not always be as tidy as you would wish.

If you are planning to buy in bulk, make sure you have sufficient storage space in the stock room, and fit strong, sturdy shelves.

It is advisable to have easy access to stock that is used daily – you may wish to have a separate area for this. A separate dispensary area is a further option.

Toilets and washing facilities

By law, every hairdressing salon employing up to five people must have a wash basin and a toilet. If you employ more than five staff, you must have separate washing and toilet facilities for each sex; and if you have more than 10 employees, you will also need to provide a separate toilet for your clients' use.

Washrooms and toilets must be well-lit and clean. Make sure you provide clean towels and soap, and don't run out of toilet paper – appoint one of the staff to take responsibility.

Ideally, washing and toilet facilities should be directly adjacent to the salon. If this is structurally impossible, do try to separate access to these areas from any other rooms where clients' intrusion could be embarrassing – particularly the staff room. If clients have to walk through a messy staff room to reach the toilet, they could be left with a very bad impression.

Specialist services

You may want to use any superfluous space to offer beauty treatments. Suggestions on this are given in Chapter 14.

The shop-front

One of the first things you should consider, as soon as you take over new premises, is your shop sign. A new one will establish that the business has changed hands, and will play a significant part in establishing the image of your salon. You may want to devise a distinctive logo for your shop sign, which will also be printed on business stationery, etc (for further details, see Chapter 11).

You could have a simple painted sign, or go for something more sophisticated, with perspex or neon lights. To find a supplier, probably the best method is to look around your area and ask other shopkeepers, whose signs you admire, where they got them from. Otherwise, look in the Yellow Pages under 'Sign makers'.

You also need to look at other aspects of your shop-front, trying to visualise it from the point of view of a prospective customer. The position of your entrance is important; it must be inviting, and there shouldn't be a 'threshold barrier', such as a solid door, or a door that sticks, which clients hesitate to cross. A central door launches the client into the middle of the salon; a door to one side of the front window is more intimate.

There is a trend towards plain glass windows, enabling passers-by to see everything that goes on inside the salon. Whether you choose to go along with this trend depends to some extent on your individual prejudices, and also on your location and clientele. Older clients in small towns and country areas tend to prefer their privacy; a frosted glass window or a blind might be more appropriate for a salon catering to their needs. On the other hand, many people do like to peer through the salon window to see what type of hairdressing establishment you're running, and to see how busy it is, before they take the plunge and make an appointment. A workable compromise is partially to screen the window – perhaps by using plants, posters, signs or photographs. You can also put a screen behind reception – don't screen off the salon completely, just provide a backdrop (which can also be used as your sales display area) to the reception desk. In this way, you provide clients with some privacy, while still giving an impression of activity to the outside world.

Music

Music is relaxing and can help to set the right mood for the salon. It acts as a 'buffer' around the client and the stylist, so that their conversation can't easily be overheard.

You must, however, select the type of music you play with the clients in mind – classical might be fine for an upmarket salon, but it's not to everyone's taste. And you are likely to find that your staff don't always want to hear the music that you have chosen; compromise is sensible, perhaps with the staff bringing in their own tapes from time to time – as long as they're not exclusively 'heavy metal'!

It is important to vary the type of music you play, otherwise it can be very irritating. If you choose the easy option and have the radio on all the time, you will find that the tempo does change during the day. But don't leave your radio tuned to a station with too many advertisements and chat shows – they can be very distracting, whereas music blends into the background. And do turn it off now and again – an occasional silence is quite refreshing.

Whether you go for radio, or tapes (with the hassle of changing them), or a mixture of the two, you will need to obtain the relevant licences to play music in a public place. Licences for taped music are available from the Performing Rights Society Ltd, 29-33 Berners Street, London W1P 4AA; tel 01-580 5544. For a radio licence, apply to the Mechanical Copyright Society, Elgar House, 41 Streatham High Road, London SW16 1ER; tel 01-769 4400.

New technology

Technology is constantly developing, and it is important for salon owners to keep up with new trends and to assess how they can help with the development and growth of the business.

For example, videos are now widely used for product promotion and as teaching aids. For apprentice training, it is worthwhile buying video cassettes covering basic colouring and perming – these teaching aids will be used over and over again for training purposes. For haircutting demonstrations, on the other hand – which will date more quickly – you can often hire video cassettes from the many hairdressing federations that now have video clubs. Additionally, the main hair product houses will come and give salon training, either by sending someone with video equipment or by providing a technical demonstration of their latest products. Your rep should offer these services; if not, contact the company's head office and enquire about in-salon training.

You might also want to investigate ways in which you could use a computer to help run your business more efficiently. There are companies specialising in computerised business systems specifically for hairdressers. There are also hair analysing computer systems available.

The annual trade fairs, in London in October and in the north of England in June, provide a good opportunity to keep up with current trends and to view the new equipment and products that are available. There are also hair shows and demonstrations all around the country, which can stimulate ideas and give a welcome boost in morale to you and your staff.

Chapter 6
Professional Advice

You should take appropriate professional advice at a very early stage – as soon as you decide to set up your own business. Although one of your reasons for wanting to run your own salon is, no doubt, the desire for independence, there are many situations – particularly in the financial and legal field – where it would be foolish to try to do without independent and expert advice.

Your accountant

An accountant will advise you initially, in general terms, on the amount of finance needed to set up a salon in your local area, and on the possibilities of raising money from outside sources. Many accountants will give an initial consultation free of charge, so it is worth approaching one very early on to assess your resources, to discuss ways of raising capital, and to decide on the most appropriate legal structure for your business (sole trader, limited company etc).

When you have found suitable premises, the accountant will help you to prepare a business plan to present to the bank manager. He or she will also advise you on the best form of bookkeeping for your salon, and set up the system for you. Thereafter, it is advisable to keep the books yourself – employing an accountant to do this is, in most cases, an unnecessary expense. You will, however, probably need the accountant to present your annual return to the Inland Revenue for tax purposes (it is not obligatory to use an accountant for this, unless you are trading as a limited company, but it is worthwhile because the accountant's figures are more likely to be accepted).

Further help that the accountant is able to provide includes advice on dealing with Customs & Excise in respect of VAT, and general business advice – such as suggestions on cost-savings.

An accountant's fee is usually based on the amount of work he or she does for you, and for a typical small salon, in the first year of trading, would probably come to about £250-£400. The fee can, however, be offset against profits for tax purposes, so the true cost to the business is lower. And bearing in mind that any reasonable accountant will save you thousands of pounds over the years, the service really is well worth it.

The best way of finding an accountant is through personal recommendation. Ask other people in the hairdressing business who they use, what services they get, whether they are satisfied, and what sort of fees they are charged. Alternatively, use the Yellow Pages – but personal recommendation is preferable, since it is to your advantage to find an accountant who is familiar with your field.

By and large, it is best to avoid big practices in town – the client pays for their prestigious city-centre offices, and they are likely to regard you as small fry in comparison with their larger and more important clients. Conversely, a one-man band is not ideal either, because what happens in the case of sickness, or holidays? Your choice of accountant should reflect the need to have immediate access to the service when you need it.

Your solicitor

It is vital to engage the services of a solicitor at the very first stages of starting a hairdressing business. He or she will advise on all the legal aspects of the initial transaction, will vet the lease and other documents connected with the rent or purchase of your premises, help with planning permission where necessary, and will also guide you away from any business practices which may invalidate your insurance.

Thereafter, you can consult the solicitor as necessary on these and other legal matters. As we explain in Chapter 8, there is a mass of legislation governing small businesses, and when in doubt, you must seek expert advice – you have too much at stake to cut corners.

Before you approach a solicitor, make a list of all the points on which you will need legal advice. This will save time, and therefore reduce your eventual bill. Ask your solicitor for an estimate of costs in advance: in most instances this should not be too difficult to provide.

As with accountants, the best way of finding a solicitor is through personal recommendation. Failing this, you can find a list of solicitors in your local library – consult *The Solicitors' and*

Barristers' Directory and Diary. It is better to use a local solicitor, as he or she is more likely to be familiar with the area and will be more accessible to you.

Your bank manager

It is a good idea to approach your bank manager very early on, before you have found premises, and to inform him or her of your intention of starting up a business. Ask if you can open a separate business account, and in preparation for raising finance, discuss the various loan and overdraft options that are available and the format in which the bank manager would like you to present your business plan.

In this way, you are thoroughly prepared. In order to borrow money, your presentation needs to be professional: approaching the bank without a plan, written documentation and a clear trading idea is a waste of time.

Your local bank branch, at which you already have a personal account, is the best place to open your business account; however, bank managers have differing attitudes towards small businesses, and if the initial reaction is unsympathetic, you might consider approaching another branch of the same bank, or perhaps, with your accountant's advice, going outside the 'big four' clearing banks.

The insurance broker

You can obtain free advice on insurance matters from an insurance broker, who will arrange the necessary policies.

You are obliged by law to have employers' liability insurance, which covers you against negligence resulting in the death or injury of an employee during the course of employment. You should also take out public liability insurance against legal liability claims by a third party (client or other person) while on your premises. This should be extended to include liability for dyeing, tinting, perming etc.

You are strongly advised to insure your premises, their contents, and stock, against damage by fire and perils – this can also be extended to include accidental damage, although there will normally be an excess charged for any claims. An important part of this cover will also be the business interruption insurance (to protect you against loss of income and rent in the event of a fire, for instance). Most combined policies also include money cover, both on the premises and while in transit. The insurance company will agree levels of benefit dependent on security. As an extension to this, there will also be personal accident assault benefits, payable in the event of a staff member sustaining injuries due to an attack while carrying money.

Remember to include glass, sanitary ware and any signs when calculating sums insured.

Do not forget that your car insurance must cover you for business use as well as the normal social, domestic and pleasure trips.

It is possible to arrange legal expenses insurance, in case you become involved in a dispute relating to fair trading legislation, the various employment Acts, or a dispute involving the purchase of goods.

Fidelity guarantee insurance is specifically designed to provide protection against theft or embezzlement of business property by an employee.

A business is dependent not only on its assets, but also on the personnel to operate it. The loss of a key person can seriously undermine a company's viability and keyman insurance is recognised as a sensible protection.

It is possible to arrange cover against death within a definite period by using term assurance. Generally speaking, the premiums have been allowed as a trading expense by the Inland Revenue and if a claim arises, the sum insured is treated as a trading receipt in the year in which it is paid. Obviously, this must be taken into account in calculating the sum assured.

There is a far greater possibility of an employee or self-employed person becoming disabled than there is of one dying before retirement age. A contract called 'permanent health insurance' has been specifically devised to provide an income payable up to normal retirement age in the event of disablement due to either sickness or accident. Normally the contract is written on the basis of the insured person being ill for four, 13, 26 or 52 weeks before the benefit begins. Where a company takes out permanent health insurance for its employees it is also possible to insure not only a percentage of the salary, but also the company's pension and National Insurance contributions.

Many insurance companies offer package policies for small businesses, combining most of the risks under one cover. This simplifies matters, as you have only one policy to renew each year, and a single premium to pay. This may be arranged by monthly instalments for a small extra charge.

The National Hairdressers' Federation and the Guild of Hairdressers offer specialised insurance schemes for their members (for further details, see below).

Other sources of help and advice

Trade associations

The National Hairdressers' Federation
It is advisable for the salon owner to join the National Hairdressers' Federation (NHF). Membership gives you immediate contact with a local area and branch network, where you can get to know other salon owners – important for picking up tips and advice, and for discussing business problems.

Membership of the NHF allows you to display the Federation's symbol on your premises – this can only help the image of your business, as the symbol is known as the hallmark of high professional standards.

Other advantages of joining the NHF, include:

- A telephone advisory service enabling members to obtain guidance on all employment and personnel matters. Representation at industrial tribunal proceedings.
- Contracts of employment at no charge.
- Free deeds of apprenticeship
- Professional advice on training, day release and apprenticeship.
- Specialised insurance schemes, designed for the hairdressing trade, with low premium rates. These are especially useful, for example, for employers' liability insurance, or for insurance against interruption of business.
- Private health insurance at reduced subscription rates.
- Free personal accident benefit.
- Convalescent home treatment.
- Salon appointment cards.
- A complimentary copy of the *National Hairdresser* newspaper (10 issues are published each year).
- The opportunity for you and your employees to participate in hair fashion demonstrations and competitions.

You can, if you wish, become a delegate to the NHF's two-day annual conference, the UK's biggest forum for master hairdressers, or stand as a candidate for area or branch office.

For further details contact: The National Hairdressers'

Federation, 11 Goldington Road, Bedford MK40 3JY; tel 0234 60332.

The Guild of Hairdressers

The Guild is the oldest hairdressing association in the country, and represents the interests of Master Hairdressers nationally.

Members are entitled to various benefits including free legal advice on employment legislation, specialist insurance at discount prices, and window stickers, certificates etc, which demonstrate the professionalism of the establishment to the general public.

The Guild sets its own examination, the Guild General Certificate of Hairdressing, which is recognised by the Hairdressing Council.

Local branches of the Guild are a forum for business, political and technical discussions, as well as demonstrations and social events.

For further details contact: The Guild of Hairdressers, 24 Woodbridge Road, Guildford, Surrey GU1 1DY; tel 0483 67922.

The Hairdressing Council

If you wish to become a State Registered Hairdresser, you can register with the Hairdressing Council if you have either:

- been engaged in the practice of hairdressing (other than as an apprentice, or undergoing a course of training) for three years; or
- completed a course of training which has been approved by the Hairdressing Council and have passed an approved examination. Approved courses of training include three-year indentured apprenticeships (with provision for day release classes at local education authority technical colleges or colleges of further education) and two-year full-time courses at local education authority technical colleges or colleges of further education.

Registration is voluntary, but has benefits in terms of demonstrating your professionalism. Articles in the press and coverage on radio and TV recommend the consumer to use *only* the services of a State Registered Hairdresser, so clearly it is to your advantage to apply for registration.

For further information contact the Hairdressing Council, 12 David House, 45 High Street, South Norwood, London SE25 6HJ; tel 01-771 6205.

Professional Advice

The Advisory, Conciliation and Arbitration Service
ACAS is a statutory independent body which, among other things, provides advisory services on employment legislation. Addresses of ACAS regional offices are given in Chapter 15.

Local Enterprise Agencies
Free advice on all aspects of setting up a small business is provided by Local Enterprise Agencies, of which there are now more than 300 throughout the country.

The address of your nearest agency can be obtained from: Business in the Community, 227A City Road, London EC1V 1LX; tel 01-235 3716; in Scotland: Scottish Business in the Community, Eagle Star House, 25 St Andrew Square, Edinburgh EH2 1AF; tel 031-556 9761.

Small Firms Service
The government's Small Firms Service can provide information, free of charge, on any type of business problem. The service also provides individual counselling sessions with experienced businessmen; the initial session is free, with a modest charge being made for second and subsequent sessions.

To contact your nearest Small Firms Centre, dial 100 and ask the operator for 'Freefone Enterprise'.

Local councils
Many local authorities are now actively involved in assisting small businesses, particularly with finding premises, dealing with officialdom, and obtaining loans or grants. Contact the local council's industrial development office (or small firms information/ advice centre) for further information.

Chapter 7
Finance and Accounting

Working out your prices

Some salon owners set their prices by comparing them with their local competitors' charges. Or if you take over a going concern, you might base your price-list on the one drawn up by the previous owner.

However, you really ought to go into the question more deeply, and base your prices on an analysis of what it costs you to run the salon and pay your staff, adding on an appropriate percentage for profit.

Basically, you are selling the *time* and the *skills* of yourself and your stylists. So if a service takes one hour of a stylist's time, you need to calculate how much it costs you to run the salon for an hour, and to pay the stylist.

Hourly costs can be worked out by calculating your weekly overheads (including juniors' wages, but leave the stylists and yourself out for the moment), and dividing by the number of hours per week you are open – say, 40. You will then know what it costs you to run the salon for an hour, before you have paid the stylists or earned a pound of profit.

You then need to calculate what you are actually paying the stylists. Work out their total weekly wages bill (allowing for holiday pay). Remember that they are not *productively* working all the time – as a rough average, 26 productive hours (out of a normal working week of 40 hours) is about right. So divide the stylists' wages by 26, and you will know how much it costs you to pay all of them to do a productive hour's work.

Then add together the hourly running costs and the hourly stylists' wages, and divide by the number of stylists. You now have a figure for 'chargeable hours', but you still haven't made any profit for yourself. You also haven't allowed for stock, so add in a figure for that. You then put on a percentage mark-up for profit – how much depends to some extent on your area – and 15 per cent

VAT. You now know what you need to charge, based on the average time it takes to carry out a particular service.

In these calculations, we have assumed that your own personal living expenses will come out of your profits. You can, however, set yourself a weekly 'wage' and count yourself as a stylist, before you add on your percentage mark-up.

When it comes to pricing retail items, take your cost price, and add on a mark-up of at least 50 per cent. This is to allow for your investment of money (when it could instead be earning you interest in the bank) and space, commission to the stylist who sells the product, profit margin and VAT.

Keeping the books

It is absolutely vital, for income tax and VAT purposes, that you keep accurate, up-to-date records. They are also important in helping you to know where you stand financially, and you can use your accounts to analyse the profitability of different aspects of the business.

There are various methods of bookkeeping, and your accountant will advise you on the system that is most appropriate for your needs. If you wish, you can employ the accountant to do all the bookkeeping for you, but this is expensive, and not really necessary – it *is* something you can do yourself. An accountant is, of course, still necessary, to monitor the system and present your accounts to the Inland Revenue.

Essentially, you must keep:

- Daily records of your sales and purchases, using a cash book
- A wages book
- VAT records (if you are registered for VAT).

Records of your takings should be entered up every evening in the cash book. It is much easier to do this on a daily basis, because if you leave it until the end of the week, it will be that much more complicated to sort out. You need either the till roll from an electronic cash register, or slips from bill pads, to record your take, and it's a good idea to break down the figure into individual stylist's takings (you will have to do this if you are paying commission). You also need to record payments you have made, including small items for petty cash (it may be more convenient to keep a separate petty cash book for these).

A small salon can enter daily sales and purchases straight into the cash book; a rather more sophisticated system is appropriate once the business starts to expand.

A wages book must be kept if you employ staff. You use it to record gross earnings (basic plus commission) for each employee, and deductions for income tax and National Insurance.

VAT. You need to complete a record of your purchases, and the VAT you pay on them, and of the VAT you have charged your customers. (We'll come back to VAT in a moment.)

Standard accounts books to keep all these records are available from stationers. Once you get into the swing of it, entering up your books becomes a matter of routine – it just seems a little complicated at first.

Banking arrangements

You should open a separate business bank account, and it is advisable to have a savings account to put money away for tax. If the bank doesn't supply a cheque card for the business account, a credit card might be useful to pay for items of stock etc.

You need to fill in and keep the cheque stubs, in order to make sure that your own records agree with the bank statements.

Taxation

Value added tax

VAT is a tax added to the value of goods and services supplied by persons and companies who are *registered* with the Customs & Excise.

You have to register for VAT if your annual turnover (that is, your takings, not your profit) is over a certain figure, or is likely to be over that amount. The level at which you must register for VAT is £21,300 (1987-88 figure) but check this, as it is uprated annually).

Below this level of turnover, it can be an advantage to register voluntarily, if you are going to spend a lot on equipment and stock to set up the business. This is because you can cut your costs by claiming back the VAT you have paid out on these purchases. However, it may not be worth it, and will involve a lot of tedious record keeping. Your accountant will advise.

VAT works like this: you charge it on your *outputs*, ie the goods and services you supply; you pay it on your *inputs*, the things you buy to run the business (stock and equipment). At the end of each tax period (usually three months), input tax – the VAT you have paid on purchases – is subtracted from the output tax you have charged your customers, and the balance is sent to the Customs & Excise. Alternatively, if you have paid more VAT than you have charged, you can reclaim the balance (this is unlikely in hairdressing, but might happen if you bought a lot of stock and equipment).

You must keep records of all the supplies you make and receive, and a summary of VAT for each period covered by your VAT return.

In the normal course of business, where you are usually collecting more VAT on your outputs than paying it on your inputs, you can take advantage of the fact that VAT is normally collected on a three-monthly basis, and in the meantime put the money aside in a bank deposit account, where it will earn interest.

Income tax

As soon as you start up in business, you should notify your local tax office.

For income tax purposes, different rules apply to:

(a) Sole traders and partners
(b) Company directors.

Most hairdressers running small businesses come under the first category, and pay Schedule D tax. This means that, unlike under the PAYE system where tax is deducted from each weekly or monthly pay packet, you pay your income tax in arrears, in two lump sums. If you choose the right 'accounting dates' (your accountant will advise you about this), you may have almost two years between starting up the business and having to pay Schedule D income tax, so you have the advantage of being able to use the money in the meantime. But do put some aside on a regular basis to cover the tax bill when it eventually falls due.

Your income tax liability is calculated as follows: no tax is payable on your personal allowance. Above this, you pay income tax on your profits, but before arriving at a profit figure, you are allowed to deduct business expenses. The expenses you can deduct are items such as rent, rates, wages and so on that we have listed under 'running costs' in Chapter 4. Keep receipts wherever you can.

You can also claim back some tax on the purchase of equipment, but the scope for this was considerably reduced after 5 April 1986.

Company directors, unlike sole traders and partners, are treated as employees of the business for income tax purposes, and taxed on PAYE. They are also counted as employees for National Insurance purposes. Limited companies are additionally liable for corporation tax.

Income tax: employees

It is your responsibility to deduct PAYE income tax (Schedule E) from your employees' wages (including overtime payments, commission, bonuses, sick pay, holiday pay etc).

Your local tax office will send you full instructions on how to calculate PAYE, and there are tables from which you can read off the necessary deductions, based on your employees' tax codes. With a little practice, this becomes a straightforward job, and shouldn't take up very much time each week.

Once a month you forward the tax deducted from employees' earnings, along with their National Insurance contributions, to the Collector of Taxes.

National Insurance

The self-employed stamp

If you are operating as a sole trader, or in partnership (*not* if you are running a limited company) you will have to pay, on your own behalf, what are known as Class 2 National Insurance contributions. (The present rate (1987-88) is £3.85 per week, but do check on the current figure when you read this, as it usually changes every year.)

You can pay these contributions by stamping a card (you buy the stamps at the Post Office) or by direct debit from your bank account.

You also have to pay a further National Insurance contribution, Class 4, currently set at the rate of 6.3 per cent of profits between £4590 and £15,340. This is collected by the Inland Revenue along with Schedule D income tax.

Employees' contributions

As an employer you are responsible for collecting your employees' National Insurance contributions, and sending them to the Inland Revenue along with their income tax and your own (employers') National Insurance contributions.

Tables are supplied by the Inland Revenue to enable you to work out the correct amounts.

Employees' National Insurance contributions are set at a certain percentage of earnings, on a sliding scale according to the amount earned (for instance, at the time of writing, employees earning between £38 and £59.99 a week pay 5 per cent, whereas those earning between £60 and £94.99 pay 7 per cent). The level of employer's contribution also depends on the amount the employee earns.

From the point of view of employing junior staff and part-timers, an important point to note is the level at which National Insurance contributions *start*, because below this, neither the employee's nor employer's contribution is payable. For people below this threshold, a modest pay rise can actually mean that they are worse off, because they are then liable for deduction of contributions.

Reading your figures and forecasting future trends

Once you have established a proper record system, it will help you to analyse the business, calculate profitability, and forecast future trends.

You will know from your records when your busiest times are, and you can arrange to buy stock just before these periods, when it will be used up quickly, rather than sitting on your shelves and costing you money.

Anticipating quiet periods is also important, from the point of view of planning promotional events – such as mail shots – to boost takings during these times. And you might want to schedule a salon refit to take place during a slack period.

You can also use your records to analyse the profitability of particular services, and calculate whether it is worth your while offering them (this is particularly useful if you branch out into new fields, such as manicure or sunbeds).

It may be valuable to analyse, in financial terms, the contribution individual members of staff are making to the business, and if you find that one person has a lower rate of productivity, think about ways in which you could improve this – by training, for example.

A computer can be helpful, both for record keeping and analysis.

Chapter 8
Legal Requirements

Running a business of any kind means taking the law into account. In hairdressing, you are concerned primarily with the legal aspects of three main areas:

- Your premises
- Your staff
- The general public.

You should engage the services of a solicitor before you start trading, and he or she will be able to provide expert advice. Additionally, the trade associations – the NHF and the Guild of Hairdressers – offer free advice on employment legislation. However, although you will probably want to seek help when you have a specific problem, it is useful for you to familiarise yourself, at least in general terms, with the basic legislation relating to hairdressing salons. In outline, this is as follows:

Premises

Planning permission
You will have to obtain planning permission from the local authority if you take over premises that haven't been operating as a hairdressing salon; permission for 'change of use' is required.

You also need planning permission for all building operations – an extension, a new shopfront, or an illuminated sign, for instance, would be covered. Always check with the local council *first*, if in doubt.

Your surveyor or architect will help you with your application for planning permission (for which you will have to pay a fee). Make sure you allow sufficient time for the application to go through, before building work begins: applying for planning permission can be a lengthy process.

Your lease
You should also go through your lease very carefully with the solicitor; you need to check on points such as whether there are any restrictions on the use of the property, and on the ancillary items you can sell; whether you are responsible for internal or full repairs; how often rent reviews take place; whether there is any control of advertising, and how difficult it may be to dispose of the lease.

Health and safety on the premises

The Offices, Shops and Railway Premises Act 1963
The Act makes provision for the safety, health and welfare of workers in offices and shops (including hairdressing salons).

You will have to register your premises with the local authority before you employ any staff, using form OSR1. You must also display on the premises a poster (OSR9) or booklet (OSR9B), providing details of the Act for the information of your employees.

The health and welfare provisions in the Act include the following:

- *Cleanliness.* Dirt and refuse must not be allowed to accumulate in any part of the premises. Floors and steps must be swept or washed at least once a week. Furniture, furnishings and fittings should be kept clean.
- *Clothing.* Space must be provided for employees to hang their clothing, and to dry wet things.
- Floors, passages and stairs must be soundly constructed, properly maintained, kept free from obstruction and from any substances that might cause someone to slip. Handrails must be provided for staircases (if the staircase is open-sided, the rail must be on that side, and the bannisters must be close enough together to stop anyone falling through).
- *Overcrowding.* Staff must not be overcrowded.
- *Sitting facilities.* Employees must have reasonable opportunities for sitting, when their work permits it, and at least one chair must be provided for every three employees.
- *Toilets and washing facilities.* Certain provisions are laid down about the number of toilets and the washing facilities you must provide (see Chapter 5).

Health and Safety at Work Act 1974
The Health and Safety at Work Act extends the scope of health

and safety legislation to all people at work (including employees and the self-employed).

The Act lays down the employer's duties to ensure the health, safety and welfare of employees at work; to conduct the business in such a way that persons other than employees (for example, visitors or clients) are not unreasonably exposed to health and safety risks; that entrances, exits and equipment are safe; to provide the necessary instruction, training and supervision to ensure the health, safety and welfare of employees; and to arrange for the safe handling, storage and transport of any articles and substances.

If you employ more than five people you will have to provide a written statement of your safety policy and arrangements, and bring it to the notice of your employees.

First aid
You must make first aid arrangements for your employees, and ensure that they are properly informed of these. (See also Chapter 13.)

Notification of accidents
If an accident occurs on your premises, and it 'disables' any employee for more than three days, or causes the death of the employee, you must notify the local authority. Written records must be kept of all notifiable accidents.

Fire precautions
There must be adequate means of escape in the event of fire, and suitable fire-fighting equipment must be provided. However, you will not need a fire certificate if you employ fewer than 20 staff (10 if you are not on the ground floor).

Shop hours
The Shops Act 1950 governs shop hours. You must close by 8pm, except on one particular day of the week – the 'late day', fixed by the local authority – when you can stay open until 9pm.

You must also close by 1pm on one weekday, under the rules covering early closing days, and you must close on Sundays.

Hours of opening may be further restricted by the local authority.

Legal Requirements

Employing staff

The provisions governing employment of staff are many, and again this chapter can give only a general outline. More detailed guidelines can be obtained from Department of Employment publications, available from Jobcentres or ACAS (the Advisory, Conciliation and Arbitration Service), who are also able to give advice on employment-related problems, and include:

No. 1. Written statement of main terms and conditions of employment
No. 2. Procedure for handling redundancies
No. 4. Employment rights for the expectant mother
No. 8. Itemised pay statement
No. 10. Employment rights on the transfer of an undertaking
No. 11. Rules governing continuous employment and a week's pay
No. 13. Unfairly dismissed?
No. 14. Rights on termination of employment
No. 16. Redundancy payments

The basic points to remember are as follows:

The contract of employment

As soon as you offer someone a job, and they accept your offer, you have a contract of employment with that person. However, it is a good idea to define the exact terms and conditions as soon as possible; and in any case, for employees who work for you for more than 16 hours a week, you must, within 13 weeks, provide a written statement of the main terms and conditions of their employment. A standard form for the contract of employment is available from the National Hairdressers' Federation.

Itemised pay statements

Each employee is entitled to an itemised pay statement showing:

- Gross pay
- Net pay
- The deductions made and why they have been made.

The purpose of this legislation is to show the employee how the figure for net pay is arrived at.

Wages Council

As noted in Chapter 9, hairdressing wages are controlled by the Hairdressing Undertakings Wages Council, and Wages Inspectors from the Department of Employment have powers to enforce the regulations and to fine the employer for non-compliance.

You must post up the notices issued by the Wages Council in a prominent position, and you must keep time and wages records for your employees for the past three years.

Holiday pay and overtime

Minimum holiday entitlement for hairdressing employees has, up to now, been laid down by the Wages Council. Under proposed legislation, however (not yet passed at the time of writing), they will no longer continue to do so, and holiday entitlement will become a matter for negotiation between employer and employee. In any case you should specify, in the written statement of terms and conditions, the amount of holiday pay to which the worker is entitled.

The Wages Council will continue to specify a minimum overtime rate. Check your current Wages Order for further information.

Sick pay

Under the Social Security and Housing Benefits Act 1982, you are responsible for paying statutory sick pay (SSP) for the first eight weeks of sickness in a tax year. You are able to reclaim the money you have paid out, by withholding it from the National Insurance contributions and PAYE income tax which is paid over at the end of each month.

Statutory sick pay is paid at one of three flat rates, depending on an employee's earnings. It is treated like wages in that it is subject to PAYE and National Insurance contributions.

Essentially, you have to pay SSP to all employees, including part-timers. There are a few excluded groups, the most notable in the case of hairdressing being those employees who earn less than the lower earnings limit for National Insurance contributions, temporary workers (under contract for less than three months) and employees over minimum state retirement age. But most other categories of employee will be eligible.

SSP is paid to employees when they are sick for more than four days in a row (including Sundays and public holidays). If they are off sick for a shorter period, no SSP is due, but you would probably want to continue paying their wages as usual, voluntarily, for an absence of three days or less.

You should let all your employees know about the days of sickness for which they will be paid. It is also advisable to agree procedures with your employees about notification of absence due to sickness – you might be content with a phone call, for instance, or you may prefer to have something in writing. After seven days' absence you have the right to ask for a doctor's certificate.

Your liability to pay SSP ends after eight weeks of sickness. After that, the employee claims sickness benefit from the DHSS.

Further information about the scheme, and the records you are required to keep, is available from your local DHSS office.

Maternity pay
A woman who becomes pregnant is entitled to receive maternity pay from her employer, provided she has been continuously employed for at least two years before the beginning of the eleventh week before the expected week of confinement. (That is, if she was working as a full-timer, which for these purposes means more than 16 hours a week – if she works between 8 and 16 hours a week she has to establish five years' service before gaining the right to maternity pay.)

Provided she continues to be employed by you until the eleventh week before the expected week of confinement (and does not resign earlier), and she gives you notice that she intends to stop work to have the baby, she is entitled to six weeks' maternity pay, which you can reclaim from the Maternity Pay Fund – the relevant forms are available from the Redundancy Payments Office of the Department of Employment.

The employee has a right to return to work at any time up to 29 weeks after having the baby. If you cannot offer her the same job, you must offer suitable alternative work. However, if you employ five people or less, you *may* be able to claim to an industrial tribunal that it was not reasonably practicable to take her back in her old job or to offer her suitable alternative work. But check with your solicitor in any case before following such a course of action.

Fair and unfair dismissal
An employee has the right not to be unfairly dismissed, and if he or she believes that this has happened, the case can be taken to an industrial tribunal.

The tribunal applies a test of 'reasonableness' to the dismissal.

The employer has to have adequate grounds to dismiss the employee, and must show that he or she has acted fairly (for instance, using the system of verbal and written warnings described in Chapter 9).

To be able to bring a claim for unfair dismissal, the employee must have been with you for at least two years. The qualifying period includes any period of notice. So, if you do want to dismiss an employee who has less than two years' service, that individual *cannot* take you to an industrial tribunal, provided that you dismiss him or her (and allow for the period of notice) before two years are up.

Dismissal on grounds such as pregnancy, or membership of a trade union, is unfair. And if you make an employee's life such a misery that he or she has no alternative but to resign, your action can be taken as 'constructive dismissal', and the employee may still be able to make a successful claim for unfair dismissal to the industrial tribunal.

Redundancy

If you dismiss an employee because there is no work for him or her, or because the business is closing down, then you will have to make a redundancy payment, provided that the employee has been continuously employed by you for at least two years (part-time workers, working between eight and 16 hours a week, must have been with you for at least five years).

A fixed scale of redundancy payments, depending on the employee's pay, age and length of service, is laid down. Part of the redundancy payment can be reclaimed from the Redundancy Fund (provided you employ fewer than 10 staff).

When a business is taken over

If you take over a salon as a going concern, and offer to keep on the staff, their employment is 'continuous', and the length of time they were employed by the previous owner is added to the time worked for you for the purposes of unfair dismissal and redundancy pay. See the note on page 85 for further information regarding such staff.

Employers' liability

If an employee is injured at work, you are usually held responsible, irrespective of whether you were personally at fault. Therefore, you are legally required to take out appropriate insurance under the Employers' Liability (Compulsory Insurance) Act 1969.

The certificate of insurance must be displayed in the salon, and you are required to record details of injuries at work in a special accident book, which is useful evidence in case of any claims. Failure to comply with the Act can result in a heavy fine.

You do not have to take out employers' liability insurance if you only employ members of your own family.

Discrimination

You must not discriminate against employees (or potential employees) on the grounds of colour, race, ethnic or national origin. If your salon has more than five employees, you should not discriminate on the grounds of sex or marital status. Women should receive the same pay as men doing work of equal value.

Freelance hairdressers

There is a distinction in law between an employee, who is under a contract of service, and an independent contractor – a freelance renting a chair, for instance, or a beautician with whom you have a similar arrangement.

The independent freelance worker does not qualify for compensation for unfair dismissal, sickness pay, maternity leave, or paid holidays, and is liable for his or her own income tax and National Insurance contributions.

This makes it attractive, for the employer, to try to reclassify staff as 'self-employed'; and workers themselves may be interested, because of the possibility of paying less in income tax. However, it isn't that easy; it depends, partly, on the extent to which the person has control over his or her own work (there mustn't be an 'employer-employee' relationship between employer and independent contractor). However, this is, at present, a rather 'grey area' – if you do plan to use freelance workers, ask your solicitor's advice.

Responsibilities towards the general public

As a professional hairdresser (which, until compulsory registration comes into force, means that you say you have the requisite skills) you have a duty of care to your clients, and in this context we must emphasise that this is particularly important with regard to the various chemicals used in hairdressing; you should always follow the manufacturers' instructions, carry out skin tests etc.

If you do not exercise sufficient care, foresight and judgement, you can be sued for negligence. This is why it is very important, when the client asks for a treatment that, in your opinion, is not suitable for her hair or skin type, and she goes against your advice and insists on the work being done, that you should ask her to write out a disclaimer, and keep this document, just in case things do go wrong and she subsequently makes a claim against you.

Because of the risk of such claims, you are required by law to take out public liability insurance. Appropriate cover can be arranged through trade associations, or through an independent insurance broker.

Trading legislation

When you sell retail items, you must comply with the provisions of the *Sale of Goods Act*. As the seller, you have three main obligations:

1. That the goods are of 'merchantable quality'. They must be reasonably fit for their normal purpose, bearing in mind the price paid, the nature of the goods and how they were described.
2. That the goods are 'fit for any particular purpose' made known to you. For instance, if the customer asks for a gel to make her hair stand on end, then it must do that – otherwise you will have to give her compensation.
3. That the goods are 'as described' – for example on the package, or display sign.

The supply of services is covered by the *Supply of Goods and Services Act 1982*. If you have agreed to carry out a service, you must do so with reasonable care and skill, within a reasonable time, and charge a fair price. If you have previously agreed a price with the customer, that price is contractually binding (you can't increase the bill, for example, because the job took longer than expected).

Also governing the relationship between buyer and seller are the Trade Descriptions Acts. These make it a criminal offence for a trader to misrepresent goods or services offered for sale, either orally or in writing. They also govern reduced price offers – so if you have a sale, or reduce your prices as part of a special promotion (say, 25 per cent off) then the higher price must have been charged for not less than 21 days during the previous six months – in other words, the price reduction must be genuine.

In conclusion, we reiterate that you should take appropriate professional advice – either from your solicitor or, in the case of employment legislation, from your trade association or ACAS.

Chapter 9
Employing Staff

Finding the right staff is vital for a small business like a hairdressing salon, where commitment is so important and the margin for error so small. Mistakes can be costly and damaging to the reputation of the business – but if you take time and trouble over the recruitment process, and are willing to motivate, train and develop your staff, you will have the right working relationships – which are one of the most important aspects of a successful small business.

Staff recruitment

Before you begin to look for a new employee by advertising, approaching the Jobcentre and so on, define your requirements carefully. With high unemployment, it is not unusual for employers to be inundated by 50 or more candidates for a single vacancy – and sifting through such a large number of applications can be very time-consuming. An accurate job description (it is simply a case of thinking clearly about the sort of person you are looking for) can save you a lot of wasted effort, and spare many of the unsuitable job-seekers disappointment.

It will help if you can specify the job in terms of:

- The job title
- The job description: a brief statement of the main purposes, responsibilities and tasks
- Terms and conditions of employment: place of work, normal working hours, pay, bonuses, holidays, sick pay, notice entitlement.

After you have done this, think about the personal attributes, skills, knowledge and experience needed to do the job. A well-tried method of organising this information is the Seven Point Plan, developed by Alec Rodger, where you consider the ideal candidate's:

1. *Physical make-up:* health, strength, appearance, manner, speech.
2. *Attainments:* education, qualifications, experience.
3. *General intelligence*
4. *Special aptitudes:* such as being good at working with the hands, or proficient at figure work (for a bookkeeper, for instance).
5. *Interests:* most hairdressers have to be able to get on well with all sorts of people. A person's hobbies or spare-time activities may indicate whether he or she is the 'social' type that you want to attract.
6. *Disposition:* acceptability, influence over others, dependability, self-reliance.
7. *Circumstances:* domestic circumstances, and how these will be affected by the job.

The Seven Point Plan will also help you to clarify your requirements when you come to interview job applicants.

Finding staff
There are a number of ways of finding suitable candidates, including:

Advertising
Advertising a job vacancy involves selecting the right medium — for instance, in the case of press advertising, the publication that is most likely to be read by the people you are aiming to attract, and that will bring in replies from the right applicants, cost-effectively.

For most small salons, the local weekly newspaper will probably be the most effective and cheapest advertising medium. Regional daily papers like the *Birmingham Post* are also worth consideration, as is the *Hairdressers' Journal*, which will of course 'target' your advertisement, reaching those who are already working in the industry.

The wording of the advertisement requires some careful thought. It is best to be fairly specific, because imprecise wording can lead to your receiving too many applications from totally unsuitable people — wasting your time and theirs. So include information about the job title (eg 'cut and blow dry stylist'), the salary offered ('top wages' tells the applicant very little), the location, conditions and any particular skills and experience required. (You can obtain help from the Jobcentre to prepare advertisements — see next section.)

Employing Staff

You could ask candidates to apply in writing, but this is not particularly recommended. A good hairdresser doesn't have to be brilliant at writing letters – and asking for written applications could leave you sifting through letters containing much irrelevant and boring information. It's probably better to give the salon's telephone number, and 'screen' applicants on the phone, if you have time. Better still, devise a simple application form (an example is given on page 82), and send it to people who ring in. You can then weed out the best applicants, whom you invite for interview.

Advertising doesn't, of course, have to be in the press. A card in the salon window or in the local newsagent's can be an effective means of advertising vacancies, particularly for apprentices or for unskilled staff such as cleaners.

The Jobcentre

The local Jobcentre can work for you in two ways:

- Suitable candidates may already be registered with the service, and will be referred to you once you notify the Jobcentre of your needs.
- A card summarising the details of your vacancy will be put on public display, and candidates may either apply to you direct, or through the Jobcentre staff.

These two services are free of charge.

There is also a job-ad service; if you need to advertise a vacancy in the press, the Jobcentre can help with writing the copy, layout, selection of suitable media and placing the advertisement; deal with telephone calls and enquiries; prepare a shortlist of candidates; and organise interviews for you. You just pay for the advertisement.

The address and telephone number of the nearest Jobcentre can be found in the telephone directory under 'Manpower Services Commission, Employment Services Division'.

If you are in the London area, you may also want to try recruiting young people through Capital Radio Jobfinder (which is part of the Jobcentre network). Capital Radio Jobfinder concentrates on finding and filling full-time vacancies for Londoners in the 16-20 age group, using radio broadcasts and a phone-in advisory service to reach young job-seekers. Telephone 01-439 4541 for further details.

The careers service

A friendly relationship with the local careers office (which helps

APPLICATION FORM (specimen)

Hair by Danielle (Your company logo)

Position applied for:

Personal details

Surname: First names:
Address: Telephone number:

Date of birth:
Nationality:
Marital status:

Education and training

(Please include short courses and day release.)

Date started   Date left   Examinations passed and qualifications

School
(after age 11):
College:
Other training:

Experience

(Start with the most recent employer and work backwards.)

Name of employer and nature of business	Dates From To	Position held	Reason for leaving

Any other information you would like to give about yourself or your experience:

References:

Signature: Date:

to place 16-19-year-olds in jobs) should be of great value for the purpose of finding apprentices and YTS trainees. To find the address of your nearest careers office, contact the education offices at your local Town Hall.

Local colleges
Rather than training your own apprentices (or recruiting through YTS), you may prefer to employ staff who have already taken a two-year full-time college course.

Word of mouth
The local grapevine – your friends and relatives, and those of existing staff – is a ready source of job applicants. Do be careful here – especially about employing members of your own family. It can lead to all sorts of trouble if things don't work out.

Private employment agencies
Private employment agencies can save you time, but they charge a fee (based on the type of vacancy, salary scale and geographical area), which can work out quite expensive. On the whole, you are recommended to try other sources first.

The interview

Once you have selected a few of the best applicants (six is often considered a good number) you can arrange to interview them. Try to schedule interviews for a time of day when the salon is not too busy – to avoid interruptions.

The fact that interviewees arrive punctually (or don't, as the case may be) gives an indication as to whether they will be good timekeepers. Do them the courtesy of being ready to conduct the interview at the agreed time – other business can wait until later.

The first thing to do during the interview is to put the candidate at ease, perhaps by asking about their journey, whether they found the salon easily etc. Then get down to the matter in hand. It may help you to prepare a list of questions in advance – using the Seven Point Plan as a guide. Try to phrase the questions so that you invite an opinion or a detailed response: begin questions with 'What', 'Where', 'When', 'How', rather than asking questions to which the candidate can simply answer 'Yes' or 'No'.

Try not to do too much talking yourself. As a rough guide, the interviewee should do about 60-70 per cent of the talking.

Make notes, either during or immediately after the interview, so that you can remember which candidate was which. Otherwise, you might start thinking, later on, 'Jane Jones – was she the blonde in the blue dress or the red-head with spots?' It's easy to confuse people if you haven't written anything down.

As well as interviewing, you will also want candidates for stylists' jobs to take a practical test. Allow for nerves here! Also, they should be notified in advance, so that they can bring their equipment, and arrange for a model (if you don't provide one).

Juniors can't be tested in this way, but you could ask them to come in for a day's trial – to see how they fit in with the other staff, and whether they are keen to busy themselves without being asked or have to be continually prodded before they do anything.

Essentially, an interview and test – or even a day's trial – is a rather hit-and-miss way of selecting a new member of staff, but no one has devised a better method. So be as fair to all the applicants and as clear-minded as you can, and assess each one carefully. Do ask for references (and follow them up) and do think about how long an applicant is likely to stay with you – the number of past jobs the individual has had is an indication of this.

After the interview, it is common politeness to let all applicants know the result – *not* just the person you have selected.

Above all, treat the interviewing and selection process as you would any major investment decision. If you pay someone £5000 a year who stays with you for three years, you will then be spending £15,000 – more if you count employment-related costs. So think about it as carefully as you would if you were planning to spend this amount of money in any other way.

Contracts of employment

As soon as you start to employ someone, you have a legal contract with that person, whether or not anything is written down. But for anyone who works for you for more than 16 hours a week, you must, within 13 weeks, provide a written statement of the main terms and conditions of their employment (pay, hours, holidays, sick pay, pensions, length of notice, job title, disciplinary rules and grievance procedures).

A standard form for the contract of employment is available free of charge from the National Hairdressers' Federation. Alternatively, there is no reason why you cannot issue the contract in the form of a letter, provided it contains all the relevant information.

Dismissing staff

'You don't want to carry someone who's not pulling their weight', comments Terry O'Mahoney. Sometimes, despite all the care you have taken with the recruitment and selection procedure, you are faced with a situation where your choice backfires and you feel you have no option but to dismiss a member of staff.

Legislation protects employees against unfair dismissal (for further details, see Chapter 8), so you have to proceed carefully. First, check with a trade association such as the National Hairdressers' Federation, with your solicitor, or with ACAS (for addresses, see Chapter 15) whether you have valid grounds for dismissing the employee.

In all cases of dismissal (except for gross misconduct, such as theft of money from the till), make sure you give the employee proper notice (if he or she has been with you for more than a month, but less than two years, one week's notice is required by law). The employee has the right to ask for payment in lieu of notice, and it is probably worth giving this, as anyone who is under notice is not likely to put very much effort into the job.

Minor misconduct, such as persistent lateness, is a common source of problems and you should follow a set procedure. Give an informal spoken warning first, and, if this has no effect, follow it up with a formal spoken warning. If the offence is repeated, or the employee commits some other form of misconduct, give a formal, written warning, and explain what will happen if he or she commits a further offence. If the employee's bad behaviour still persists, you should then give a final written warning, and if this does not solve the problem you can then proceed to dismiss him or her.

It is important to keep copies of all written communications with the employee (and keep a record of oral warnings, too) in case he or she eventually takes the case to an industrial tribunal. However, the best way of avoiding any of the problems associated with unfair dismissal is to make sure that all procedures are fair, well understood and closely followed.

Note: if you take over a going concern, you may not be happy about the existing staff, or you may need fewer staff because you are reorganising the salon. However, you are obliged by law to take on the existing staff. Remember, too, that the continuity of the business will be affected if you don't take them – they will have built up relationships with clients, who are quite likely to follow them to other salons. It is tempting to try and get round this legislation by arranging for the vendor to make the staff redundant before the sale goes through. But according to ACAS there should be a 'genuine redundancy situation'; if it could be proved that redundancies took place purely because of the sale of the business, claims for unfair dismissal could be upheld. Take legal advice in any case.

Methods of staff payment

Wages Council

Minimum wage rates in hairdressing are set by the Wage Council, which also lays down regulations concerning overtime rates. You must pay the minimum rate; you can't get round the regulations by making a private agreement with an employee.

When you start up a completely new salon, you should contact the local Wages Inspectorate and arrange for copies of the Wages Orders, which set out the current minimum rates, to be sent to you. (This will happen automatically if you take over a going concern.) The addresses of the Wages Inspectorates are given on p. 131.

You must keep time and wages records for three years, to show that you are observing the provisions of the Wages Order, and you must also post up notices issued by the Wages Council in a prominent position where all the workers affected can read them.

You can, of course, pay above the minimum, and in that way be able to attract and keep better staff. You may wish to introduce some form of bonus or commission scheme for stylists, based on a percentage of their takings after VAT. You must, however, make sure that they are paid the Wages Council minimum every week – irrespective of the amount of work they do. So you need to pay at least the Wages Council minimum as a basic, and commission or bonus on top.

Employees under 21 are no longer entitled to Wages Council minimum rates. You are able to pay what you like, but if under 21s do receive low pay, make sure that you provide good training to compensate.

Check information on minimum rates and other terms and conditions by referring to your copy of the Wages Order.

Weekly or monthly pay

Whether you pay weekly or monthly is up to you. Paying on a monthly basis involves less work, since there are only 12 wage packets per year to make up for each employee, as opposed to 52.

But generally, it is easier for lower-paid staff to manage their money if they are paid weekly. There is no reason why you can't, therefore, pay the juniors at the end of each week and the more senior staff on a monthly basis.

You *must* supply an itemised pay statement – and you can pay in cash, by cheque or direct debit. If you pay in cash, giving crisp new notes (in small denominations) is a nice touch.

If you want to change either the method of payment or the intervals at which you pay (from weekly to monthly, for instance), then you must give your employees prior notice, and get their agreement to the new system.

Tips

Since tips are an important part of staff wages, it is important that each individual should keep his or her own tips, and a fair division made of tips that are given jointly to stylist and junior.

Keep individually marked boxes on the reception desk for each person's tips. Don't interfere. However, you could point out to your staff that it is in their own interest to keep a record of how much they receive in tips, and to keep receipts for any equipment they buy, in case they wish to query their tax codings. Tips are taken into account by the Inland Revenue when setting PAYE tax codes for hairdressers, but there have been cases where individuals have been able to prove, by keeping records and showing receipts, that their coding is incorrect.

Communicating and motivating

It is essential to have a happy atmosphere in the salon – petty grievances, if not dealt with quickly, can soon build up and sour relationships between staff, or between staff and owner.

Regular staff meetings are a useful means of keeping the channels of communication open, and dealing in a fair way with any grievances that arise. Brenda Bond says that she has staff meetings about every four to six weeks, at which she'll say, 'This, this, and this has annoyed me.' She explains, however, that 'Very rarely do I point a finger at any one person – they usually know who it is who has had too many phone calls, or is popping out for breaks too often.'

As well as reprimanding the staff for any misdeeds, the owner should, of course, praise where praise is due (both at meetings and on a day-to-day basis). But be careful of favouritism – you must be seen to be fair.

Sometimes it can help to have separate meetings for stylists and juniors, if there is conflict between them and you want to get to the bottom of it. It can also help to see staff individually from time to time, to discuss their work, training, pay reviews and so forth. You might like to do this in the form of an annual 'appraisal interview', in which you discuss with each employee, in some depth, that individual's:

Personal qualities
- appearance
- personal organisation (whether the individual is methodical, punctual and adequately equipped)
- care of salon property
- relationships with customers, superiors and other staff
- ability to self-motivate
- additional expertise
- efficiency of reporting

Effectiveness in sales and salon operations
- telephone contact (efficiency, manner)
- pricing of work (correctness)
- commercialism (how effectively the member of staff sells the salon's services)
- attitude to change
- achievements (weekly targets, increased takings)
- stock control
- application of skills attained
- updating of product knowledge

You can grade these points on a sliding scale, and use the assessment to create an awareness in the individual of his or her strengths and weaknesses, and areas in which there is room for improvement. The aim of an appraisal interview is not to criticise in any negative sense, but to help each member of staff to see the ways in which he or she is making an effective contribution, and to motivate them to improve their performance.

Staff incentives
One way of encouraging staff to sell more of a particular product is to organise some form of incentive scheme, possibly linked to a special promotion organised by the manufacturers. For instance, one company organised a promotion whereby staff collected bottle tops from its shampoos, and exchanged a certain number

for an LP. More generous prizes include vouchers which can be exchanged in part-payment for a package holiday.

Schemes like this obviously benefit the manufacturers, but your own profit increases too, if sales go up. You might also like to organise your own promotion of, say, a slow-moving line that you want to get rid of, or of a particular salon service such as highlights. Set a target, and offer prizes to staff if they sell that specified number of products/special services.

Incentive payment schemes like commission or bonuses are also obvious motivators. But non-cash incentives like prizes of various sorts, and birthday gifts, can also help to boost morale.

Training is, of course, another excellent way of motivating staff, particularly if you demonstrate your commitment to them by investing money in sending them on external courses. Entering competitions, too, creates involvement and boosts morale – especially if one of your stylists wins. Pay expenses, to encourage your staff to enter externally run competitions.

At Christmas time, you need to do something extra for the staff. A Christmas bonus, even if it isn't very large, is the best way of showing your appreciation of good work. You could also take the staff out for a meal, and buy small gifts. Another activity at Christmas time that creates involvement – and client interest – is the hairdressers' tradition of fancy dress on Christmas Eve. You can work to a particular theme – the staff of Through the Looking Glass dressed up as 'Heavenly Bodies' in 1985, the year of Halley's Comet. Dressing up like this is great fun, and it also gets your salon talked about – which is obviously good for business.

Management incentives

If you employ a manager, incentives of a more serious sort need to be considered. Profit-sharing is an obvious one; also the offer of a partnership. You could also consider arranging an occupational pension scheme, or private health insurance.

Employing specialists

You may find it advantageous to hire a specialist – a manicurist, beautician, Afro stylist, tinter/permer or make-up artist – either full time if the amount of work justifies it, or part time (on your busy days) or on a rent-a-chair basis. Advertise through the usual channels.

Rent a chair

Freelance stylists and specialists who have their own clientele, but need premises to work in, may be attracted by the rent-a-chair arrangement. For a flat rate, the salon owner hires out a working position, and the services of the salon (including appointment taking). Sometimes the flat rate payment takes into account the stock used, or it may be charged as an extra.

The freelance stylist works on a self-employed basis and pays his or her own income tax and National Insurance, and VAT if applicable (you are not liable for VAT on the freelance's takings). He or she should also have separate insurance to cover industrial accidents (if totally freelance), but if you are subcontracting the work, then you are responsible for insurance. Check on the differences with your insurance broker.

Chapter 10
Training

The value of training

In an industry where success depends almost entirely upon having a skilled and highly motivated workforce, the importance of training cannot be over-emphasised. After all, as a salon owner, you are basically selling hairdressing skills – those of your workers and yourself – which the population at large lack. If cutting hair was something anyone could do, then there would be no demand for hairdressing services.

A high level of hairdressing skill demands a corresponding level of training. No one can afford to be complacent about their abilities – there is always more to learn. That is why training should be an ongoing process, continually updating your own skills and those of your employees.

A good initial training at the start of a hairdressing career is, of course, an absolute prerequisite. Though the details of apprenticeships, college courses and private hairdressing schools will no doubt be familiar to the experienced hairdresser, we have outlined them in this chapter for the sake of those who are new to the business – non-hairdressers who want to invest in a salon – and who need to know how the various schemes work either from the point of view of recruiting trained staff, or alternatively in order to equip themselves with the basic skills.

A further type of training, which more and more salon owners are coming to appreciate, covers management skills – anything from the basic nuts and bolts of running your own business to more advanced courses on marketing, PR and staff motivation. Being a good hairdresser does *not* necessarily mean that you will be good at running your own business; and there are now a number of courses which help people to make the transition from hairdresser to business proprietor.

Initial training

Apprenticeship
There are various means of acquiring a basic grounding in hairdressing skills. The traditional method is via a three-year apprenticeship. During this period, a young person is employed by the salon.

A young person starting work in a salon is not automatically an apprentice – an apprenticeship is an official contract which must be drawn up in writing, and be properly executed.

It is usual for a new, junior employee to work in the salon for a short probationary period before the apprenticeship itself begins. If both employer and employee are suited, then an indenture (the formal term for an apprenticeship agreement) is signed by the employer, the apprentice and the apprentice's parent or legal guardian. Standard forms for indentures are available from the National Hairdressers' Federation.

During the three-year apprenticeship period, the employer has to provide training. In a good salon, this will include practical experience in every aspect of hairdressing, plus evening training sessions (model nights) to teach cutting, tinting etc. In addition to receiving training in the salon, the apprentice can attend a local technical college for one day week, to learn the more theoretical aspects of hairdressing. He or she can then take the City and Guilds of London Institute examination in hairdressing, and if a pass is obtained, can go on to do a further advanced course.

Note: after 1989-90 there will be a new Hairdressing Training Board/City and Guilds qualification.

Full-time college course
As an alternative to an apprenticeship, there is a growing trend for young people with exam passes to take a two-year full-time college course. These courses usually include practical hairdressing experience in the college salon, as well as the more theoretical aspects. Some colleges arrange practical work experience in nearby salons.

Most full-time college courses give a very good grounding in basic hairdressing, and are recognised by the Hairdressing Council as the equivalent of an apprenticeship. (However, not all salons find college courses as acceptable as an apprenticeship.)

Both apprentices and college leavers are employed, in their first year after qualifying, as first-year operators, before becoming acknowledged as stylists.

Private hairdressing school

The third method of training – an intensive course at a private hairdressing school – usually lasts for between six and 12 months. Fees tend to be high, and a further disadvantage is that their diplomas are not recognised by the Hairdressing Council. However, having said that, for adults who are new to hairdressing, they offer a rapid means of learning the basic skills, and since it is not essential, at present, to have any particular paper qualifications to set up a hairdressing business (even though the industry is pressing for some form of compulsory registration) they could offer a good way in for the non-hairdresser who aspires to owning his or her own salon. For such an individual, a private school offers the further advantage of enabling you to take a course in one particular aspect of hairdressing, such as cutting and blow drying – which would save time (and money), especially if you plan to employ other stylists who have had the traditional all-round training.

Some private schools also provide 'refresher' courses, which are useful for people who have been away from hairdressing for some time, or to give an update on methods of styling and working with hair. There are also short courses appropriate for improving the skills of first-year operators, and any other hairdressers or beauticians at any stage in their careers, when they need to be motivated by new ideas.

Youth Training Scheme (YTS)

Many hairdressers are now recruiting all their junior employees through YTS, which has clear financial advantages. The scheme lasts for two years and provides the opportunity for trainees to gain a recognised qualification. From 1989-90 the National Preferred Scheme, now widely used for YTS training, is to be extended and will become the nationally recognised vocational qualification for the hairdressing industry. It will be awarded jointly by the Hairdressing Training Board and City and Guilds.

During the two years, trainees will receive at least 20 weeks of out-of-salon training, but the rest will be in salon, with the youngsters learning through work experience, and making an active contribution to your business.

YTS is administered by 'managing agents'. As a small employer, you would work with a managing agent by providing the on-the-job part of the training programme. The managing agent will want to agree with you how the training programme should be organised, and to arrange to review the training and record the progress made.

YTS trainees can either be employed directly by the salon, or be 'unemployed'. The unemployed trainees are paid a weekly allowance by the managing agent, who also decides when they are available for work experience. The chief advantage, from the employer's point of view, is that there is no commitment to employ these trainees after the programme ends.

If, on the other hand, you employ your YTS trainees, you are paid the weekly allowance by the managing agent, and you are responsible for paying the trainee's wages, which must be *at least* as much as the YTS allowance. The chief advantages of 'employed YTS' are the freedom to recruit a young person from any source, rather than just through the managing agent, and the ability to pay a higher salary to encourage the trainee to remain in the job.

It is possible for an employer to transfer an unemployed trainee to employed status at any time during the programme; you could start off with 'unemployed' trainees, and if their work is satisfactory, then employ them.

You can get in touch with your local managing agent by contacting the careers office, or the nearest Manpower Services Commission Training Division Area Office (address in the phone book under 'Manpower Services Commission').

Adult training

It is worth noting, while on the subject of MSC-sponsored training, that there are also courses for adults, run at the MSC's Skillcentres, under the Job Training Scheme (formerly TOPS). The 30-week basic hairdressing course is available (at the time of writing) at the Glasgow, Felling, Leeds, Liverpool, Rochdale, Birmingham, Leicester, Letchworth, Medway, Enfield, Cardiff, Bristol and Portsmouth Skillcentres. An extra nine weeks, covering perming and colouring, is available at some of these centres.

The course is designed to train people who have little or no experience of hairdressing, and provides a good basis for them to build on through further experience in a salon.

The cost of the training is covered by the Manpower Services Commission, and trainees receive an allowance to live on while taking the course.

In-salon training

A hairdresser should never stop learning, and you will want to keep *all* your staff up to date and knowledgeable about the latest trends. Staff training can take the form of weekly meetings for the exchange of ideas, and demonstrations – either using video or with the staff watching you or another stylist working on a sample head.

For training purposes – demonstrations and staff practice – you will want to attract models. Advertise your model nights, offering free haircuts or give-away prices.

You may also want to take advantage of manufacturers' offers of in-salon demonstrations, to show the staff how to use new products, or update their knowledge of existing products. There may, too, be trendsetting salons in your area which, for a fee, will provide haircutting and styling demonstrations on your premises.

You can also arrange specialist teach-ins on other subjects, such as sales techniques, henna application or make-up, run by the manufacturers.

It is interesting and morale-boosting for staff to attend outside shows or demonstrations every now and again. Turk Mahmoud recommends that 'you ought to go to at least six shows a year – one every couple of months. You see work and then you adapt it to your own particular market.'

Business training

Starting a business involves acquiring all sorts of new skills to deal with problems such as marketing, bookkeeping, personnel etc. The time-honoured method of learning these was through experience – you started up and either sank or swam. Nowadays, however, you can increase your chances of success by taking one of the many courses that are now available for people starting up their own businesses.

There are plenty of evening classes and short courses, provided by adult education institutes, polytechnics and colleges of further education, aimed at people who are thinking of starting up their own businesses (not specifically in hairdressing – it could be any type of trade) and who want to explore the possibilities, and find out about raising money, looking for premises, presenting a case to the bank and so forth.

There are also free, full-time and part-time courses in setting up a small business, run by the Manpower Services Commission.

Their 'small business programme', aimed at people who plan to employ several staff, consists of about 15 days' learning about business management (pro rata on part-time courses) followed by individual market research on participants' own proposals (a grant is available to help with this), and then individual review sessions during the first few weeks when the business is in operation. (Further information is available from your local Manpower Services Commission Training Division Area Office.)

There are also many organisations in the hairdressing field running courses in business management. Wella UK, for instance, have a four-day 'staff trainer' course, L'Oreal provide three management training courses (in costing, staff motivation and training the instructor), Alan International are currently opening a new academy which will provide business lectures, and Clynol, together with the consultancy firm, International Salon Management, are running courses on promoting the salon, staffing and financial management. In addition to the courses they run with Clynol, International Salon Management also offer management training packages for salon owners, and other services such as PR and management consulting for the hairdressing industry. There is also 365 Hairdressing, which offers an ongoing education and motivation package for the organisation's members, and other courses in budgeting and marketing for non-members.

Of course, you also learn about management all the time, from experience; and don't forget that a good accountant, and other small business advisers (covered in Chapter 6) are a valuable source of information.

Beauticians

If you plan to open a beauty salon offering facials and skin care, you will need to employ a qualified beautician.

The question then arises of what 'qualified' actually means. The problem is that this is a rather grey area – there is no single recognised method of training, and some students qualify as beauty therapists, rather than as beauticians. However, a student who has taken a course at a college of further education will have received fairly extensive training, and students from private colleges who have passed the examinations of the International Health and Beauty Council, the Confederation of International Beauty Therapy and Cosmetology, the International Therapy Examination Council, or CIDESCO will be soundly trained.

Chapter 11
Marketing and Selling

The importance of an image

The way you project your business – the salon's appearance *from the outside*, clients' impressions inside when they are being attended to, and contacts beyond the salon (through advertising and promotion of various kinds, as well as your own personal contacts) – all go to create a particular image for the salon. This should be related closely to the type of clientele you want to attract, and you should already have established who they are in the course of your market research, before taking over the salon. You need to aim at a definite segment of the market: you can't be all things to all men.

Of course, it is by your standards of hairdressing that the reputation of the business stands or falls, and every possible attention should be paid to maintaining the quality of the service, by employing good staff and providing regular training sessions for everyone, not just for apprentices. However, there is a great deal you can do *in addition* to promote your business and to attract (and keep) a good following.

The appearance of the salon – from the pavement, where the prospective client sees it – is of tremendous importance. The colour, layout and typeface of your shop sign should be in keeping with your image (and with the design of your business stationery). Your window is one of the best means of promoting the salon, free of charge. You can screen it off and use it to display retail items and promotional material supplied by the reps; or, if you prefer, leave the area uncluttered, so that passers-by can see in and gain an impression of activity – which in turn draws in more custom. A busy salon is its own best advertisement.

You can also paint on the window (rather than on your shop sign) the type of service you offer – for instance, 'Hair Design for Men and Women'. If this lettering is at eye level, it will probably be more noticeable than the shop sign itself. And you might also want to display your price-list in the window (this is very much a matter of personal taste, and depends also on the area and type of clientele, but it can be effective in drawing people in).

When you're considering the outside appearance of the salon, don't forget the entrance, which must be inviting. A solid door is normally bad for trade – you need a door that can be seen in through, even if it's not entirely glass.

Once the client walks into the salon, what happens? Try it yourself and picture where you would stand, whether you would feel comfortable, whether the general impression is of ordered efficiency, and style – in short, is the ambience welcoming?

The staff have a key role to play in presenting the right image, and the importance of their having attractive hair, clothes and make-up almost goes without saying. Their attitude, too, in terms of the way they welcome clients, their general friendliness and aptitude for dealing with people, are also vital if you want to build up good relationships, and develop the steady, regular repeat business which is the mainstay of any salon. As Terry O'Mahoney says, 'If you've got the right personality, that goes a long way in hairdressing. A friendly hairdressers has a lot going for it.'

However, when you start up a new salon, you have to do a little bit more than just open the doors and smile welcomingly in order to tempt people in. You will probably want to plan some kind of initial launch – it needn't necessarily be a very grand affair (in any case, you probably won't be able to afford to splash out, having used up most of your spare cash on decorating and equipping the premises). A small party, however, is a good idea. Robert Neill launched his second salon with a wine and cheese party, to which he invited regular clients from his other salon, and the local shopkeepers he'd got to know while the premises were being done up. (It's always worth getting to know the people from the other businesses in the area – as well as being able to help out in emergencies, they can be a good source of trade.)

You may also want to announce your opening by advertising, or by getting editorial coverage in the local newspaper. We shall come back to the whole question of advertising and public relations shortly, but before you think about planning an advertising campaign, you need to consider whether to adopt a logo (symbol) to identify the salon – which can then be used on all advertisements and other printed matter, as well as on gowns and other salon equipment.

Choosing a logo

A logo gives the salon a corporate identity, and catches the eye when used in advertising. It isn't necessary to have one, but it does improve the appearance of stationery, own-brand products etc.

A logo could be a design based on a pair of scissors, or pieces of hair, or male and female figures seated back to back (to signify that the salon is unisex). If your salon's name consists of initials, you could arrange these into a distinctive symbol. Alternatively, you could simply use the salon's name – in a particular typeface which is always the same on the shopfront, stationery and promotional items – but this is not a logo as such.

You can design your logo yourself, or ask a friend to help you. Alternatively, either your signwriter or local printer will be able to help. The important thing, however, is that everything should co-ordinate, and your logo is stamped on all the signs and printing connected with the business – this gives a very professional image. So *either* agree on a logo with your signwriter, and then present the same design to the printer, *or* get the printer to produce 'artwork' (a layout showing the logo and salon name, as you want it to appear on your stationery) and then arrange for the signwriter to paint the same design and lettering on your shopfront.

If you want a really professional job, you could commission a graphic designer (found from the Yellow Pages, or from *The Creative Handbook*, which should be available in your local library), but this service does not come cheap.

Your logo can appear on your: shop sign, stationery, own-brand packaged merchandise, gowns and towels, sweatshirts and T-shirts, and promotional give-away items such as book matches, pens, pencils, plastic carrier bags, badges, balloons for children.

Checklist of printing requirements

You will need to ask a local printer, or quick-print shop, to print at least some of the following items:

- business cards
- appointment cards
- letterheads
- labels for own products
- price labels
- promotional handout leaflets
- price-list

- posters and display signs – hours of opening, special offers etc
- promotional items
- receipts and other stationery for accounts – eg VAT receipts, daily or weekly takings sheets.

If you are short of cash, a company stamp can be used for things like letterheads and receipts – but it doesn't look so professional. While on the subject of costs, do remember, too, that colour printing will be more expensive than black and white.

Promoting your services

Hairdressing nowadays is a competitive business, and it pays to advertise and promote your salon. You may just happily jog along without doing any advertising, but if you have a clear, well thought out promotional strategy – not just from time to time, but on an ongoing basis – you will reap the benefits in the form of increased turnover.

A word on definitions, first of all: *promoting* the salon involves adopting a whole approach towards the business, and tailoring it to your clients' needs. You should know what market segment you are aiming at, and whether your prices and services are compatible with your 'target' group. You must know your local area intimately, and be aware of new developments – the construction of a new office block, for instance – which could affect the social composition of the locality. You must also know your competition, and keep one step ahead of it.

Your staff, too, should understand why you have a promotional strategy, and you need to train them so that they can sell your services and products effectively.

Advertising plays an important part in promoting the salon, but there are also other ways in which you can get your name known. Articles in the local press, radio spots – any mention at all in the local media is great publicity if you can get it. Your salon's outside appearance, as we have already discussed, is probably the most important image-builder. Special offers and promotional discounts (eg 'two for the price of one') can tempt people in. And then there is anything you can do to get the salon talked about – word of mouth is the best form of promotion.

Paid advertising is obviously a good idea when you start up a brand new salon, or take over a place which has been run down, but you shouldn't necessarily see it as something to do only when you're getting the business off the ground. A regular, planned advertising campaign, with proper monitoring of the results, can pay off in the longer term.

You might consider advertising in the following media:

1. *The local newspaper, or freesheet.* It works best if your ad appears at the weekend, when people are more likely to be thinking of having their hair done and have time to ring up and make an appointment.

Display advertisements work best, and should, for maximum impact, be placed on a regular basis, not just as one-offs.

When wording your advertisement, think carefully about what you want to achieve. Before the business starts up, you could place an 'opening soon' advert, possibly linked to some form of discount or special offer for readers who cut out the ad and bring it with them. You should set a time limit for this – 'valid until such-and-such a date' – otherwise you could find people coming in months or even years later with the same clipping.

Giving a discount or special offer to people who bring in the advertisement has the advantage of enabling you to monitor the results of your advertising campaign in a very direct way. You can keep a careful record of the number of people who bring in the advertisement, and compare the number of new clients gained with the cost of advertising.

Another way of assessing the effectiveness of your advertising is to ask clients, when you complete their record cards (see page 113), how they first heard of the salon. Periodically, you can then assess the effectiveness of your advertising by counting the number of clients who mention it, and comparing this with the cost of your overall advertising campaign.

Advertising in the local press can be geared to special events, such as Valentine's Day, the Christmas party season, or summer holidays. If an article on hair or beauty appears at the same time, so much the better.

2. *Local radio.* This is a way of reaching a large audience, but can be relatively expensive. The advert must be repeated to be effective.

3. *Yellow Pages/local directories.* This is a particularly good means of advertising in an area such as a holiday resort, with a high volume of passing trade. Don't bother about advertising in purely 'trade' directories: these are mostly used by the manufacturers to sell to *you*.

4. *Cinemas.* Cinema advertising can be relatively cheap, and cost-

effective if you have a long contract. But make sure that the cinema that you choose is fairly well attended by the type of people you wish to attract.

5. *Billboards on buses, parking meters, council litter bins*, etc. These can be a cheap and effective means of advertising – but your ad must be of good quality, and be regularly changed.

Other ways of promoting your salon, at a price, include:

6. *Leaflets*. An attractive, well-designed leaflet can be distributed to local houses, either by a firm of leaflet distributors (find them through the Yellow Pages), by the local newsagent's delivery boys (or girls), or, at a pinch, by your own staff, though this is a rather wasteful use of their time. Leaflets can also be handed out in the street, to selected members of the public (eg women in the 20-30 age range).

7. *Free-standing advertising boards* on the pavement outside the salon. An expensive means of drawing attention, particularly if your premises are somewhat inaccessible (on the first floor, for instance). Be careful not to cause an obstruction.

8. *Mailing or telephoning previous clients* – with reminders, plus possibly vouchers, special offers etc. Handled carefully, this can be a very successful way to secure future business. A word processor/microcomputer is helpful for mailing.

9. *Birthday/Christmas cards and free gifts*. These are all good ways of building client loyalty. Gifts can be inexpensive – diaries and flowers, for example. Cards, especially birthday cards, need a good record system – again, a computer/word processor would help.

Public and press relations

So far, we have considered ways in which you can promote the salon by spending money – and in many cases, the response can be measured in terms of cost-effectiveness; if you monitor your advertising or leafleting, you can say that by spending x amount of money, you have attracted y number of clients.

There is, however, another rather more nebulous area – that of public and press relations – over which you have less direct control, but which can project your image, and get your name known in the local area.

Any editorial coverage you can arrange in the local paper is bound to attract interest. You could, perhaps, arrange some special event – such as a marathon haircutting session in aid of charity – which the local paper would be keen to cover. Or you might contact the editor of the women's page and offer suggestions for articles on hair and beauty care. It very much depends on the paper whether this will actually be followed up, but it is worth a try.

Discounts and special offers

It is a good idea to offer a discount when you introduce a new service, to encourage new and existing clients to try it out. It could be tied in with your advertising, as we have already suggested, with clients bringing in a voucher or coupon.

Many salons offer lower prices on quiet days, sometimes for specific groups such as old-age pensioners, students or the unemployed. The only snag with this is that it *could* have a negative effect on your image; for instance, if you are aiming at a young, fashion-conscious market, the presence of old-age pensioners might cause surprise, to say the least. So do consider the implications carefully.

Another scheme that can help to draw in new clients is the 'bring a friend' offer, where you provide a special deal (eg two for the price of one) when a client introduces a friend. This can work very well; friends *sell* very effectively to each other. It helps to build loyalty, as well as introducing new business. But it can be expensive, and needs careful control (eg through an effective system of client record cards) if it is to work properly.

You can also offer some form of loyalty bonus to existing clients, in the form of vouchers or stamps that clients collect at each visit, eventually building up to a free session. This provides a strong incentive for clients to return, but could have the drawback of 'cheating' – again, it needs careful monitoring.

If you wish to encourage clients to bring their children, you can offer special prices, obtain child-sized chairs and offer a few gimmicks such as free badges or a 'first haircut' certificate. It helps, too, to provide children's books and toys, and if space permits, a crèche.

Client competitions

Every so often the manufacturers of hairdressing products organise competitions, as part of their overall marketing back-up service. They supply entry forms, prizes (such as holiday vouchers), posters and promotional aids. The competition forms usually ask the entrants to write down the type of product that has been used, and the name of the salon – so from the manufacturer's point of view, it is a way of building up their mailing list, as well as having the obvious benefit of selling more products.

From your point of view, encouraging clients to enter these competitions can help to boost sales, as well as to generate client interest in the products supplied.

You can also run your own competitions. Through the Looking Glass had one in which the staff were asked to bring pictures of themselves as under fives, and of their mothers, and clients were asked to match the mother and daughter, the prize for the most successful attempt being a promotional sweatshirt. An event like this creates a talking point – outside the salon as well as inside – and anything that generates interest like this is good publicity.

Photographs
A professional photo session can produce favourable publicity, but it is expensive, and it can be difficult to produce your best work in the unfamiliar atmosphere of a photographic studio. You need to plan carefully, engage a photographer with a good portfolio of hair and fashion shots, and agree an all-in rate of payment with him. Use a professional photographic make-up artist, and professional models, if possible.

There are photo seminars available, run by the leading manufacturers such as L'Oreal, Schwarzkopf and Wella, for hairdressers who want to observe a photo session in action and find out about the best techniques for preparing models for the camera and planning a session.

You can also produce photos of your work much more cheaply, using amateurs – who may be willing to do the work for free, in return for materials and pictures for their portfolios. These photographs may be sufficient for displaying your own work in the salon, but might, on the other hand, go disastrously wrong! You lose very little, however, and an amateur session could be a way of experimenting with photographic work before going on to a full professional session.

Alternatively, you can buy posters to illustrate contemporary styles from wholesalers, manufacturers or through trade magazines.

Chapter 12
Buying Stock

Right from the start, you will need a certain amount of stock – perms, tints, conditioners, shampoos, styling mousse and so forth – both for use in the salon and for your customers to buy and use at home. It is important, however, not to have too much money tied up in stock, especially at the outset when you are operating on a limited budget.

Decide how much you can spend – as a rough guide, you should not have more than 80 per cent of a week's takings tied up in stock. Don't buy too many different products at the start – you'll need to test them out and see which ones are most suitable for your type of work.

Buying in bulk, although it is often cheaper in the long run, is not advisable at first, until you have established a pattern of trade and can see which items are most commonly used. It is not normally possible to obtain a refund on products that you can't sell – so just purchase small quantities until you know precisely what you're going to need.

Choosing your suppliers

Stock can be bought either from wholesalers or direct from the manufacturers, via their sales reps.

Wholesalers (often referred to as 'cash and carries') offer a wide range of products from different manufacturers. A visit to the wholesaler's warehouse can be useful if you want to buy in small quantities, or if you want to try out different manufacturers' products. You might, however, get 'finger happy', and end up buying more than you budgeted for, so do make a list and stick to it.

Alternatively, if you have a large order, you can telephone the warehouse and have the goods delivered to the salon. And some wholesalers have representatives, who will call and take your order.

Manufacturers also sell directly to salons. You can arrange for their representatives to call – although you will probably receive unsolicited visits in any case.

Representatives, of course, only sell the lines that their particular company produces, so your choice is more limited than if you go to a wholesaler. There is often a minimum limit, too, on the size of order – for instance, one manufacturer stipulates that you must buy at least £20-worth of goods. However, there are certain advantages in buying directly:

- Some manufacturers offer special discounts: usually, the more you buy, the bigger the discount. (If you are friendly with another salon owner, you might be able to combine your orders to obtain a larger discount.)
- From time to time certain products are offered cheaply, as part of a special promotion. It can be worth buying when this happens, provided you can afford to have the money tied up in stock. (You have to be careful here, and calculate whether it wouldn't be cheaper in the long run to buy the same product in smaller quantities from a wholesaler – having the use of the money in the meantime.)
- Manufacturers' reps provide sales aids such as leaflets, posters and competition entry forms, which can be helpful for promoting retail lines.
- Reps can also give you up-to-date information on new products, and they will organise in-salon demonstrations, free of charge. This is a service which is not available from wholesalers.
- Certain manufacturers make a commitment to sell their products only to professional hairdressers, not to other retail outlets. So if your clients want to buy these products, they have to come to you.

Remember, when you're deciding where to buy your stock, to allow time for the manufacturers' orders to arrive, and don't wait until you're down to your last bottle of a product before you reorder.

Most hairdressers do, in fact, buy their stock from a variety of sources. So experiment with different suppliers, and see which ones suit you best.

Personal experience

Turk Mahmoud has some wry comments about reps. 'It all sounds very good, when the reps come in', he says. 'There's a very clever salesman in this area. He offers six weeks' credit, and *says* it's a good deal, but we've then found that we're overstocked. And if stock isn't going to turn over, it's not worth having it sitting around for months. Sometimes, we find we get better individual deals from the cash and carry.'

Own-brand packaging

Once your salon is established, you might want to go in for own-brand packaging – printing your salon's name on the retail items you sell. This is good publicity for the salon, gives you a professional image, is an effective way of establishing customer loyalty, and also helps to increase profits.

Companies which offer own-brand packaging can be contacted at trade fairs, or you can find them through a trade directory. It generally takes about four weeks for orders to be completed.

Before ordering own-brand supplies, do test the product out in your salon first, and make sure you've done accurate costings.

Methods of payment

Any credit terms that you can negotiate will obviously be helpful. Some wholesalers and manufacturers will allow you up to 30 days to pay, as long as you are able to supply a credit reference.

This is not always possible, however: some suppliers ask for pro-forma payment (goods are paid for before the order is despatched). Or you may have to pay on a cash-on-delivery basis.

A few smaller suppliers offer a discount for prompt payment. To take advantage of this and any credit terms you have been able to arrange, do keep an accurate record of all the bills you receive, and note the dates when payment is due.

It is also advisable to check each order when it arrives, making sure that the goods delivered are the ones you asked for, the quantities are correct, and that you have been invoiced for the right amount. Mistakes can and do happen, and you'll find it very difficult to sort out what has gone wrong once the goods have been put on the shelves with your existing stock.

Stock control and rotation

You can save time and money by having efficient methods of stock control. In the first few months, try to write a daily list of the stock you have used. This will enable you to know exactly what to reorder, and when to do so – with the result that your system will run smoothly, and you will not be wasting money by having it tied up in slow-moving lines.

As new stock comes in, move the old stock forward. Make sure you move stock through the retail sales area, too – nothing looks worse than products sitting on shelves and gathering dust.

Boxes of new stock, bought in bulk, should be labelled with their date of arrival, so that you can check how long it takes before their contents are sold. You can then calculate whether any discount you received was worthwhile, or whether it would have been more cost-effective to buy smaller quantities, at a higher price, and to have invested the money in some other way.

Your stock room should be well organised, so that you know at a glance when you need to reorder, and so that your yearly stock-taking causes the minimum amount of fuss and trouble.

It may be convenient to have a separate stock room which can be locked up, to store items bought in bulk, and an additional stock cupboard for small quantities of products you use on a daily basis. As well as making it easier to find items that are frequently used, this also helps to reduce the risk of petty pilfering. For security purposes, make sure, too, that your employees are aware that you have a system of stock control, and that you know exactly what the stock levels should be.

When you're ordering stock, beware of fads and trends – you don't want to be left with unsaleable goods on your hands. You need adequate supplies of whatever is in demand, but beware of over-ordering items like hair paints, which are very much a nine-day wonder. Be careful, too, about stock for which there is a seasonal demand. If you sell accessory items like clips and bows, bear in mind that these tend to be bought at two distinct times of the year – before the summer holidays or before the Christmas party season – and adjust your pattern of ordering accordingly.

Resist the temptation to use new products before you've finished up the old ones. New items always seem more exciting, and the staff will want to try them out – but do make sure that any old stock that you want to use up is out of the way first. Then, and only then, make sure that staff are aware of the new products, and know how to use them.

Manufacturers will supply information on the shelf-life of their products. You may have a problem, however, if you take over an existing salon and there is old, undated stock. If in doubt, don't use it – although the manufacturers are usually very willing to test out a sample, to see if it is still safe.

Occasionally, you will come across the situation where a customer wants to return a retail product. It is advisable to replace it, whether there's anything wrong with the product or not, in order to maintain goodwill. If products are sub-standard, the manufacturers are in any case normally willing to provide you with replacements.

Personal experience
When Christine took over her salon, she discovered items in the stock cupboard that were at least 30 years old! She showed them to the manufacturer's rep, who was so fascinated that she took some of them to display in the factory as 'museum pieces'.

A few items are still usable – Christine has discovered a market for pre-war hairpins which, with changing fashions, are once again in demand.

Stock-taking
Stock-taking has to be done annually, to provide a 'closing stock' figure for your accounts, and for insurance purposes. All the stock should be removed, and the stock room cleaned.

You might find that a microcomputer would help you to keep accurate stock records. With computers, though, it is very much a case of 'garbage in, garbage out'. In other words, the computer can only help if you have given it the correct figures to work on in the first place. You'll need to devote some time to learning how the computer works, and then, once the system is up and running, you need to feed in all the necessary information.

Trade shows and exhibitions

It's not really necessary to go to trade shows and exhibitions, and it may be difficult to do so if you live a long way away. But if you can attend them, these events are a useful means of keeping up with styling innovations and new hairdressing products. It's too easy to stagnate, to get stuck in a rut – you do need to get out and about sometimes and check what other hairdressers are doing.

Another way of keeping in touch with industry trends is through your trade association, which will put you in touch with other salon owners. Meeting other people in the hairdressing business and discussing common concerns, is a valuable way of keeping oneself up to date.

Details of hairdressing functions are regularly listed in the *Hairdressers' Journal*.

Chapter 13
The Daily Operation of the Business

It is mainly through experience that the owner of a hairdressing salon learns about the day-to-day running of the business. Each salon is different, and every owner will have unpredictable circumstances to contend with. Nevertheless, there are some general points that can be made about the most effective ways to communicate with clients, to sell your services, deal with complaints and crises, ensure security, and generally run the business with maximum efficiency.

Communicating with clients

Effective communication is one of the key aspects of success in the hairdressing business. It is not always easy to interpret a client's wishes, particularly if they are badly expressed, but the hairdresser's skill at understanding a person's real needs – and state of mind – is one of the crucial elements in achieving customer satisfaction.

You and your staff must talk and *listen to* the clients. Communication starts as soon as a client steps through the door of the salon, with the receptionist (or other member of staff) greeting the client by name (a system of client record cards, described on page 113, will help you to remember names) and generally adopting a welcoming tone.

Before carrying out any operation on the hair, it is good practice for the stylist to talk to the client about the desired style, and, if possible, to make physical contact – by brushing the hair, for instance. This creates an important 'rapport' between stylist and client. Through experience, the stylist becomes skilled at interpreting signals at this point – for instance, the client might say 'I think I just want a trim', but expressed in a certain tone, accompanied by appropriate gestures, the real meaning might be: 'I'm fed up with my appearance; what are you going to do about it?'

Facial expressions, too, are indicative of a person's true

opinion. An experienced hairdresser can tell from a glance at the client's face whether he or she is really satisfied with a new style – regardless of what the client actually says.

A salon owner or manager should always keep an eye open to check that all is well, and if you see that a stylist is having problems with a client, you need to find a discreet way of interrupting and making sure the client does not leave the salon dissatisfied.

There are certain easily recognised categories of client. For instance, there is the client who will always be a bit disgruntled, whatever you do. There is the one who will buy anything new, regardless of cost. Then there is the overstressed client – perhaps a harassed mother, for instance – who comes to the hairdressers' to relax; and the person who wants to save money, who can be 'sold' a product or service if you are ingenious enough to think of ways in which it will actually lead to a saving in the long run (eg a better perm will last longer). There is a training video called 'Client Approach', available from Wella, which illustrates these various client types, and suggests appropriate responses. It is a useful aid for training staff in human relations.

Listening carefully to any comments that clients make can help you to improve your business, to promote its good aspects and eliminate the bad ones before clients vote with their feet and go elsewhere. For instance, a client might ask if she can sit away from the window. If she does, try to find out why she wants to move – it might be that a little more privacy, perhaps created by a screen – would be more suitable for your particular area.

Another instance where you should take note of client feedback is the question of providing free tea and coffee. You might want to charge for hot drinks, but if clients comment that your competitors provide them free of charge, consider changing your policy. Otherwise, it could be a needless bone of contention.

This type of feedback from clients is particularly important in the early days, when you are trying to establish the business. Really listening to clients' comments, and putting right any negative points, could make all the difference between having a flourishing salon and just scraping by – or worse, going out of business altogether.

As well as making sure that you really listen to your clients, and explain your products and services to them, make use of visual media for selling purposes. Place sales display stands and product show cards provided by the manufacturers to the best advantage, where everyone will see them. You can also create awareness of new products by using styling units for sales displays (though the drawback to this is that you may be making it more tempting for the light-fingered to walk off with a couple of bottles, and it might create clutter). But stickers, strategically placed on all your mirrors, can be a good way of promoting a product. Through the Looking Glass achieved very encouraging sales of designer perms by this means.

Client record cards

For a number of reasons, it is helpful to maintain a system of client record cards. Each card should record the client's name, address and telephone number, together with details of each appointment, the type of service supplied, details of any products used (tints, perms) and their effectiveness.

New clients should be asked to complete the card on their first visit, and you may also want to ask them how they first heard of the salon, to check the effectiveness of your advertising and publicity.

You can use the client record cards for a number of different purposes. You can organise mail shots with details of special offers, you can send each client a Christmas card (perhaps with information about discounts to create more business in the quiet period after the Christmas rush), and you can send regular clients cards on their birthdays and other special occasions (such as weddings or anniversaries). It is also helpful, when a client comes in for an appointment, to be able to look at the record card beforehand and remind yourself of how long it is since you last saw the client, and how much time has elapsed since a perm, or other special treatment, was done. This gives a personal touch (the client, naturally enough, assuming that you remember all the details) and can be a boost to sales.

If you have a receptionist, she should take responsibility for filing and updating the cards. Otherwise, a junior could be given this task. Whoever looks after the filing system should look in the appointments book each morning and take out the cards for the day. In the evening, she should check that they have been filled in and put them back into the main file. It helps to have two record card boxes to simplify this job.

On the other hand, you may decide to get a computer to organise your client record card system. With its aid, more complex tasks, such as sending regular reminders to clients when appointments are due, or forecasting the level of future business, are made much easier. In theory these jobs can be done manually, but are rather a chore, taking valuable time from other activities.

Appointment books

Keep whichever type of appointment book is most convenient – loose-leaf or bound. You can use the appointment book to keep a record of staff hours of work, which is required by the Wages Council.

Awareness of client purchasing power

As the owner of a hairdressing business, you should be aware of the potential of the local market for hairdressing products and services. You should be aware of what segment of the market you are aiming at, and tailor your services accordingly.

There may be all sorts of 'extras' that could boost your turnover, which you may have overlooked. For example, everyone washes their hair, so every client is a potential purchaser of shampoo and conditioner. You and your staff are the best people to advise clients on the most suitable products, and you should capitalise on this – most sales of hair products are through chemists, so there is a whole market there for you to capture.

There is also a market for brushes and combs, and a seasonal demand for items such as Christmas gift sets. People are going to buy these things somewhere – why not from the hairdresser?

Being aware of clients' purchasing power also means that you should have some idea of how much the client can afford to spend. Obviously, there is some leeway in this, and if the client can be persuaded that a new hairstyle will be as much of a boost to her confidence as a new outfit, then you should be able to persuade her to spend more on hairdressing services. But every market has its limitations, and you may, depending upon your area, decide to go for volume and speed rather than quality and high prices. In that case, you will want to schedule appointments at very frequent intervals, to use the cheapest products, and to rely on a quick turnover of a large number of clients to produce your profits. It is very much a case of tailoring your services to meet market requirements.

In-salon entertainment

All the extras you offer to clients – magazines, tea and coffee, food if you provide it, music (radio or tapes) and video – come under this heading.

The quality of these services should be as high as that of your hairdressing. Magazines should be the latest issues, not last year's. Tea and coffee *must* be fresh and hot. Some salons provide snacks of various kinds, such as sandwiches or salads. If you plan to offer these, check first with the local authority that you are complying with the hygiene regulations, and that offering food does not constitute any 'change of use' to your business premises.

Videos are becoming a popular way of illustrating new styles. A video screen in your window, catching the eye of the passer-by, is an excellent way of creating interest and drawing people into the salon. Or you could use it inside, for customer entertainment and hair education. As a growing trend, with the expansion of video entertainment, has come a new gimmick: many fashion shops and large stores have access to regularly changed in-house informative videos. Some top hairdressers are now introducing this new medium, and it will certainly have repercussions in the trade. You will, however, need to obtain a licence from Phonographic Performance Ltd, Ganton House, 14-22 Ganton Street, London W1V 1LB; tel 01-437 0311, in order to play video tapes in a public place.

Licensing also applies to the playing of recorded music (tapes and records) and the radio – see Chapter 5.

Dealing with customer complaints

From time to time you will inevitably have to deal with complaints from dissatisfied clients. Try to do this tactfully but firmly, and above all remember that the reputation of your salon is at stake.

Some clients are dissatisfied with their hair, it may be because of stylist error, or because they insisted, against advice, on having a treatment or style unsuitable for their particular hair type. (It's better not to do the style in the first place, and encourage your staff to get management permission if they're asked to do something which goes against their better judgement.) If the stylist is at fault, it is best to have the hair re-done immediately by someone else, and to make sure that the person who made the error is given appropriate guidance or training. If having the hair re-done is not acceptable to the client, you can offer a refund – but unless you issue a disclaimer, you are admitting the fault by doing so, and also running the risk of the client going to another salon to have the hair put right, which is bad for your image.

On the other hand, if the stylist did nothing wrong, there are various courses of action open to you. You can either re-do the hair, or ask the client to go home and think about the new style, and to come back later if she is still dissatisfied (there is a risk, here, however, that you could lose her). You could offer a refund, but this might be exploited by a client who is determined to avoid paying the bill (there are people who complain, just to see what they can get away with).

For anything more than a minor complaint, try to persuade the client to accompany you to the quietest, most private place in the salon, so that normal business is not disrupted, and other clients are not given a bad impression. Ask the client to sit down for a moment, and if you can, busy yourself and keep him or her waiting for a few minutes. A pause gives time for the person to calm down, and when you return, they will be sitting and you standing, which gives you a slight psychological advantage.

Do everything you can to put right any faults, free of charge. As a last resort, you can offer the client's money back, but as this is tantamount to admitting to poor workmanship, think carefully before doing so. If you are not at fault, write out on a slip of paper that you are refunding the money but you are not admitting to faulty work, and ask the client to sign it. This is then a disclaimer, in case the client should take you to court.

Damage to your clients' clothing can occur because of mishaps during chemical processes. Obviously you should take great care that this doesn't happen, and if clients are wearing expensive outfits, encourage them to change into dress-type gowns. If you do have an accident, offer to pay the customer's dry-cleaning costs and/or offer reasonable compensation (your insurance will cover this). A thoughtful gesture after the event – such as sending a card and a bunch of flowers to the client's home – can help to remove any remaining ill-feeling.

You should take all reasonable safety precautions, but if an accident does happen, treat the situation with care. Don't automatically accept liability for an accident, or for loss or damage of a client's property. For instance, if someone claims to have lost one of their personal possessions in the salon, make every reasonable effort to find the missing item while the client is on the premises, but if you don't find it, don't accept liability – suggest that the client *may* have left it elsewhere (at home, perhaps).

With any serious complaint, write down exactly what happened, as soon as you can, so that should the client decide to take legal action, you have a record of your side of the argument. Find witnesses to back up your case. It is to be hoped, however, that serious problems of this nature will not arise. Most complaints can be dealt with by prompt, tactful and diplomatic action on your part.

Crises

Crisis management is probably a major part of any salon owner's job. When something goes wrong, you're the one that has to sort it out, and fast, if business is not to be affected.

The major things that can go wrong are mainly either to do with your mains supplies – water, electricity and gas – or with your staff.

As far as the supply of water and power is concerned, problems may be beyond your control, perhaps because of a strike, or something like a burst pipe. There is, however, a lot you can do to minimise the inconvenience to clients. In the case of strikes, for instance, prior notice is usually given, so you have time to re-schedule the appointments of those clients you are able to contact.

It helps to have a back-up water heating system in case of power failure or problems with your boiler. This is discussed on page 51.

Frozen water pipes are often a problem in winter time. Pipes should, of course, be well lagged and insulated, but if in spite of your precautions they do freeze, check carefully for bursts or loose compression joints, especially in places where there is likely to be trouble – close to an exposed wall, for instance. If a pipe is damaged, or if you are in any doubt, turn off the nearest control valve and call a plumber. Otherwise, thaw the pipe out slowly with cloths soaked in hot water, or with a hairdryer.

Remember that even if the electricity or water supplies are cut off, you won't necessarily have to close the salon. Some hairdressing operations can be carried out in daylight, without electricity. And if you are without water, check with the Water Board on the extent of the affected area – it may be that your neighbours haven't been cut off, and with willing hands to carry buckets, you can get hold of sufficient supplies to keep going temporarily.

Whatever the crisis, your main priority must be your clients. *You* may be in a state of panic, but make sure, before doing anything else, that you explain what's happened and apologise profusely to clients for any inconvenience they may have to suffer. Offer to make alternative appointments if possible.

This applies in the other common crisis situation: staff shortage. When this is caused by illness, there is normally no prior warning, so if the staff who have turned up can't cope with the workload, you must re-schedule appointments, taking care to explain to clients why this is being done, and to apologise for the inconvenience.

When staff have had to take on extra work because of a colleague's absence, or some other crisis, do make sure that you reward them for having coped with the situation – even if it's only with a word of thanks.

Regular salon requirements
Handling cash on a daily basis
You have to establish procedures for handling cash, for maximum security and efficiency. If you can afford it, an electronic cash register is a good investment (it can be leased, rather than bought). As well as being a secure way of holding money, the electronic till has the advantage of automatically giving you a print-out of the day's takings, which can be broken down by operator (each person having a code to use when they ring up the till). This considerably simplifies the bookkeeping process – if you don't have an electronic cash register, you will have to rely on manual methods such as bill-pads.

If you leave cash on the premises overnight, it should be put in a safe or other secure place known only to you. It is possible to buy safes that are 'disguised'; there is one on the market, for instance, that is designed to look like a large electric socket.

Cash that leaves the premises at the end of the day's business should either be removed by you personally or put into a bank night safe. If one of the staff is responsible for taking money to the bank, emphasise to her that should the worst happen, and she is held up or threatened, it's better to give up the money than to risk getting hurt. To minimise the dangers, don't publicise the fact that cash is being taken to the bank, and try to vary the times at which it is removed from the premises.

On busy days, it is perhaps worth cashing up half way through the day.

Other money problems
Wrong change. In principle, the customer is always right. You should always follow the practice of putting a large note on top of the cash register until you have counted out and given the change, but if mistakes do, nevertheless, happen, you can cash up instantly, and see if you're holding more than the balance indicated by

the till roll. But this might be inconvenient if you're busy. It's easier to make an arrangement to phone the client at the end of the day, after you've cashed up, or, if the person really insists that the change was wrong, just to give them the money.

Returned cheques. If a cheque is returned by the bank, it should not cause problems if your client record cards are up to date. You can write a polite note to the client, explaining what has happened, and ask her to pop in and pay.

In any case you should really only accept cheques that are backed by a cheque guarantee card, and train all staff to verify that the signature, date and cheque card number are correct.

Laundry

In a small salon, it is cheapest and most convenient to wash and dry your towels and gowns on the premises. Use a good quality soap powder and fabric conditioner to make towels last longer.

For preference, towels should be dried naturally on a clothes line. If outdoor space is not available for this purpose, you could at least save on drying costs by hanging towels on a clothes horse overnight, before finishing them off in a dryer.

At a pinch, you can use the local launderette if you haven't got room for your own washing machine, though you need to establish a good relationship with the owner. Remember, however, that constant trips to the launderette will be an extra cost, in terms of lost staff time, as well as launderette charges.

A larger salon would either have a separate laundry room, equipped with commercial-sized washing machines and dryers (either leased or bought outright), or would bring in towels from an outside laundry.

Cleaning

Cleanliness is extremely important, not just from the point of view of health and safety, but also because most clients are likely to be quite houseproud themselves, and will notice any dirt or dust immediately.

Every staff member should take pride in having a clean working environment, and it's good policy to make everyone responsible for cleaning up after themselves, rather than leaving the job to the juniors.

There are, however, major cleaning jobs, like the floors and washrooms, which should really be done when the salon is empty. It is probably simplest to employ a cleaner for a few hours a week to cope with this work. The alternatives are to set aside a time – when you are closed – for all the staff to muck in together and clean up; or to ask one member of staff (usually a junior) to stay behind and do the cleaning (and give them time off in lieu).

Controlling salon costs

You don't want to seem petty or mean, but nevertheless a careful watch on seemingly small items can save you hundreds of pounds over the years.

Careless use of products can mean that you are literally pouring money down the drain. You could check on the amounts of shampoo and conditioner your staff are using and, with their co-operation, work out possible savings.

Most salons have stock that they no longer use, that is too good to throw away. Use it, don't waste it – perhaps it could be sold to another salon, or used by the junior staff for practice on model nights.

The telephone also offers potential for major cost-savings. If your staff use it for private calls, a separate telephone book should be used to log their calls, which should be paid for. It may be easier to control telephone costs by installing a payphone for staff and client use.

Probably the area with the greatest potential for saving money is salon maintenance. Any item that is slightly damaged – a chair with a tear in its upholstery, for instance, or a small corner of wallpaper peeling away from the wall – should be repaired immediately. You should make regular checks of salon decor and equipment, and it is worthwhile cultivating a local handyman who will call and do minor repairs, almost immediately. Electrical or gas fittings should, of course, be left to the professionals – but the odd-job man can do all the other little things you would never otherwise get round to – saving considerable sums (through avoiding the necessity for major repairs) in the long run.

Salon security

If you are worried about the possibility of burglaries and break-ins, ask the advice of the crime prevention officer at the local police station.

Shrinkage (petty theft)
Unfortunately, there is a strong possibility that you will lose some

items of stock and equipment through pilfering (the polite term in business is 'shrinkage'). This is a common problem, and although the single items themselves may be of low value, when you add them up, they can amount to quite substantial losses.

It is difficult to eliminate pilfering altogether, but there are a number of ways in which you can reduce it.

In the case of staff, you can remove both the opportunity and the temptation to steal by having an effective system of stock control, and asking staff to sign for products as they use them. You can also sell retail items to your staff at cost price, allow them to use salon services like sunbeds free of charge, and to have their hair done for nothing. If it is easy for them to have access to the salon's services and stock cheaply and legally, there is less temptation, and less need for stealing.

Security can also be improved by giving staff their own lockers for personal possessions, and making them individually responsible for small items of equipment they use, such as hand-held hairdryers.

It is also important to make the rules about use of stock absolutely clear when new staff join you.

Never, never, accuse a member of staff of stealing unless you are 100 per cent sure that you have caught the right person. But if you *are* absolutely certain, then prosecute. If you don't prosecute, but dismiss the worker and explain that you did this because they stole something, you could be sued for defamation.

When it comes to pilfering by clients, again the solution is to minimise temptation and opportunity. It is easier to spot when items of stock are missing if they are displayed in the manufacturers' point of sale stands – you can see at a glance if anything has disappeared. Make the receptionist, if you have one, responsible for retail sales.

Sadly, clients do sometimes take retail items and other odds and ends such as towels, soap and toilet paper. Reduce the temptation as much as you can by having clear, ordered displays in the salon. If you catch a client red-handed, it is probably better to say something like: 'Did you want that bottle of shampoo? I'll put it on the bill', rather than make an outright accusation. And in the washroom, it may be worth installing a hot-air hand dryer and a soap dispenser, if you find that towels and soap disappear.

The security of clients' personal possessions, such as coats, is discussed on page 46.

Safety and first aid

Commonsense safety precautions include the following:

- Make sure gas and electrical appliances are installed by qualified fitters, and regularly serviced.
- Never touch switches or electrical appliances with wet hands (water conducts electricity).
- Don't have flexes trailing across the floor, which could cause someone to trip.
- Check that there is adequate lighting on stairways.
- Place damaged or unsafe appliances out of the way until they are repaired, so that they cannot be picked up and used unawares.
- Make sure you have a fire extinguisher.

The local fire prevention officer at the fire brigade will be able to help if you have any cause for concern. (Larger salons, employing more than 20 people – or 10 if you are not on the ground floor – need a fire certificate from the local Fire Authority.)

Organise fire practices as part of the salon training programme. Fire drill should include the immediate switching off of power supplies, and it is also worth making sure that the staff know where the main water stopcocks or taps are, so that they can also turn off the water supply if necessary.

It is desirable for at least one member of staff to be trained in first aid. Courses are provided by the St John's Ambulance Brigade and the Red Cross, or (in Scotland) the St Andrew's Ambulance Association.

Every salon should have a first aid box, kept in a prominent place known to all staff. If the salon has five employees or less, the first aid box should contain:

- a card giving general first aid guidance
- 10 individually wrapped adhesive dressings
- 1 sterile eye pad with attachment
- 1 triangular bandage
- 1 sterile covering for a serious wound
- 6 safety pins
- 3 medium-sized sterile unmedicated dressings
- 1 large sterile unmedicated dressing
- 1 extra large sterile unmedicated dressing

Tweezers and scissors may also be useful.

Chapter 14
Forward Planning

Future expansion

It is not necessarily the best hairdressers who succeed in the business – it is good hairdressers who combine their skills with business acumen. It is important to keep your eyes open all the time for new business opportunities. You can look at ways of increasing profitability by doing what you do now – but better. You may find ways of boosting your takings by promoting retail sales, or by offering a health or beauty service. It may be possible to extend your premises to cope with a greater volume of work. You may reach a point, however, at which you have exhausted the possibilities of your existing salon and need to think in terms of opening a second one, if you wish to keep growing.

Increasing the efficiency of the business

You can increase profitability by doing what you are doing already – ie running a single independent hairdressing salon – but sharpening it up and doing it more effectively.

You can concentrate on boosting sales – perhaps by doing less of the day-to-day hairdressing yourself, and spending more of your time on promoting the business, using the various methods suggested in Chapter 11.

Additionally, any steps you can take to reduce costs – by a careful analysis of things like telephone bills, laundry charges, or the maintenance of the salon – will increase profitability. So, too, will innovations that save time – one of your most valuable assets – and allow your staff to cope with a greater volume of clients. For instance, if bookkeeping and administration take up time that could otherwise be devoted to clients, it may well be worth investigating the possibility of speeding up these tasks by using a computer.

Another way of cutting costs is to sublet any unused space you have – a basement, for instance, could be rented out to another business.

A second salon

Before you open a second salon, you need to be sure that you have a firm financial base on which to expand. You should really be making sufficient profit from your original business to be able to cover the running costs of the new one during its early stages, until it begins to break even and show a profit. Your accountant will advise you on the appropriateness and timing of the move.

It will, of course, be easier to borrow money to finance a second salon, since you will have the assets of the first as security, and – more importantly – you will have established some kind of track record upon which the bank manager can assess the viability of your new proposal. Staffing, too, should be easy – indeed the ready availability of good staff is sometimes the reason for opening a second salon. As Brenda Bond explained: 'You create a lot of staff by training – and we suddenly found that we were slightly over-staffed at our first salon, so I thought it was time to open up a second.'

One problem, however, for the owner, is that you can't be in two places at once, and expansion necessitates the appointment of a manager to run the second salon. Once you have a manager, you must be prepared to delegate, and this can be difficult for the small business proprietor who is used to making all the major decisions alone. But you have to allow the manager a certain degree of responsibility – he or she shouldn't have to refer every minor day-to-day decision to you.

If you grow even bigger, and operate a chain of salons, having the right management will become absolutely crucial, as you will find yourself increasingly involved in administration and paperwork.

Running two or more salons in the same area can have tremendous advantages. Your name becomes known, and clients who move from one part of town to another will probably prefer to go to another branch of the same business, rather than to a completely unknown salon. You save on costs such as advertising, and you can buy stock in bulk. If the two salons are close by, the 'overload' from one on busy days can be coped with by the second. Altogether, it means one thing: greater profitability.

A beauty salon

The number of hairdressing salons which offer a beauty service is growing, not surprisingly, given the recent 'health and fitness' boom, and the fact that beauty treatments are a natural complement to hairdressing. Each has a spin-off effect: beauty attracts more clients to the salon, and hairdressing clients may overcome any inhibitions they have about visiting a beauty salon if the service is offered alongside hairdressing. There is still a feeling, among some members of the general public, that visiting a beauty salon implies there is something physically *wrong* – whereas a combined hair and beauty salon has greater psychological acceptability.

A big plus about beauty treatments, for the owner of a hairdressing salon, is that they can be offered on a very limited scale initially – to 'test the water' – and the service can then be expanded if it shows potential. If you are thinking of trying out the market, then you could start by offering:

1. *A range of retail beauty and skin care products.*

2. *A make-up service.* Unlike skin care treatments, this does not have to be carried out by a fully qualified beautician. Instead, stylists or receptionists can take one of the beginners' make-up courses offered by the main cosmetic suppliers, which are regularly advertised in the *Hairdressers' Journal*. The suppliers are often able to provide sales aids such as display materials and client literature, and may also advise on lighting and layout of the make-up area.

The amount of space required for a make-up area is minimal – no more than a styling unit. It is advantageous, however, to place the make-up service at the back of the salon, or to screen it off, to allow for privacy.

3. *Ear piercing.* This involves very little capital outlay, and has the potential for a high profit margin. An additional advantage is that very little space is required – all you need is a height-adjustable stool or chair which will enable you to pierce at ear level.

Legislation was introduced in 1982 to make the process of ear piercing safer and more hygienic, and equipment manufacturers responded by developing disposable cassette systems, which have all but eliminated the risk of infection. The equipment can be inexpensive, though quality varies. The price charged to the client depends very much on the area. You can also tap into the market for earrings and jewelled studs, thus adding to your profits.

4. *Eyelash and eyebrow tinting.* The equipment needed is minimal. You, or one of your staff, can easily learn all you need to know by taking a short course – the suppliers will put you in touch with organisations providing training.

5. *Nail extension and manicure services.* You can find out all about these from the product manufacturers, who exhibit at the major trade shows. They may also run short courses – Revlon, for example, who are one of the leading companies in this field, do so.

All these services can be carried out in the hairdressing salon itself, and involve a very modest investment in terms of equipment and training. You might want to send your least busy stylist, receptionist, or one of the juniors on a course, so that they can make an additional contribution to the business. If the services you offer prove successful, and you have space that is not being fully used, you might want to go one step further and set up a separate beauty treatment room. For this, you will need at least 10 by 7 feet of space – for a fully extended treatment chair, beautician's stool, trolley and other equipment (eg steamer). The room should have a hand basin, power points and a good lighting system (with dimmer switches).

With these facilities, you will be able to offer facial and skin-care treatments; but you will, for these services, have to engage a qualified beautician. You might prefer, rather than employing someone directly with the consequent charge on your overheads, to rent the space to a self-employed beautician, or come to some form of profit-sharing arrangement; but you *must* have someone who is properly qualified to provide the treatments (for beauty qualifications, see Chapter 10).

Profitability on beauty services is generally rather lower than on hairdressing. Nevertheless, it can provide a good, steady source of income if you sell 'blocks' of treatment (at a slight discount), which will create client commitment.

Rules and regulations
There may be local bylaws governing the registration of beauty salons (it depends very much on the area) and you may be required to pay an annual registration fee. Contact the environmental health department of the local council *before* you make any definite plans – you need to get their go-ahead first.

An advisory service is available for beauticians and beauty salon owners who join the British Association of Beauty Therapy and Cosmetology.

Personal experience
Robert Neill recently invested about £1000 in a beauty section for

his new, second salon, and has employed a qualified beautician who trained at the Shaw College of Beauty Therapy. He finds that the beauty business has a seasonal pattern: 'The summer months were very good, but then there was a lull, and towards Christmas it became busier again.'

'I don't think you really earn a great profit out of beauty, because prices are relatively low,' Robert feels. 'Even West End prices for beauty treatments are quite cheap, if you take into account the amount of time you're spending on each person.'

Nevertheless, he feels that it is a good service to offer, if you have the space available. He's noticed the spin-off effects, with clients who come in for hairdressing then deciding to have a facial, massage or manicure.

Sunbeds

Another popular service, which can be offered either as an adjunct to a hairdressing salon (without beauty) or as part of a separate beauty salon, is sun-tanning. This, again, will need space – you will need private cubicles for the sunbeds, and although a shower is not a legal requirement, it is practically essential. A sun-tanning service also involves considerable investment – prices range from £400 to over £14,000 – and staff training is essential (the Association of Sun Tanning Operators provides short courses).

Sun-tan lamps emit two types of ultra-violet light – UV-A (cosmetic tanning rays) and UV-B (burning rays). There are two main types of fluorescent lamp used in sun-tanning equipment:

1. Lamps that give out mostly pure UV-A rays (with a UV-B output of less than 0.5 per cent). If used correctly, these lamps carry almost no risk of burning.
2. Lamps with a higher UV-B output, that are said to give a very fast tan, but carry associated risks of burning and long-term skin damage.

It can be very difficult to distinguish between the two types, but you must insist, when buying a sunbed, that the UV-B output is 0.5 per cent or less. You should also check that the tubes are of a reputable make, and that there is a well-designed reflector which deflects light on to the body.

Do make sure that the equipment, once installed, is regularly checked for mechanical and electrical safety, and that it is regularly serviced. Follow all the recommended procedures – clients *must* wear goggles, and these should be disinfected after each client has used them. (Or each client can buy an individual pair.) Clients should remove perfume, deodorant and make-up before going on the bed (this is one reason why a shower is necessary) and they should take out their contact lenses. There are also certain circumstances in which it is not advisable to use a sunbed – during the first 12 weeks of pregnancy, for instance, or if someone suffers from a heart condition or is taking certain drugs which can sensitise the skin. This must all be carefully checked before the client uses the bed.

Don't exceed the recommended exposure times, and make sure the time switch is accurate. After use, clean the sunbed thoroughly. Clients will probably want cold drinks, and showers to wash off perspiration. You will have to allow for the extra laundry charges – in terms of towels and robes – when working out your costings.

Some local authorities require sun-tanning establishments to be licensed, and there may be requirements about ventilation and fire doors – check with your local council before you install any equipment.

Further information is available from the Sun Tanning Advisory Bureau.

Trichology
A further additional service is trichology (the treatment of diseases and disorders of the hair and scalp). You have to be qualified to practise as a trichologist, and this usually takes three years of part-time study. There are a number of technical colleges offering courses, or you can take the Institute of Trichologists' correspondence course.

Retailing
Most salons sell a range of hair products, and this is a useful sideline. If you want to expand the retail side of the business, you could sell jewellery (perhaps in conjunction with an ear-piercing service), cosmetics, or health products. If space is available you could even sell clothes, or expand, perhaps using an adjacent shop, into the boutique business.

Anticipating problems
Running your own business brings with it a mass of problems, and there is always a risk that yours could be among the one in three new businesses that are estimated to fail. You can reduce,

though not eliminate, the risks by careful planning, monitoring and control; by being a good manager, in other words. You need to anticipate trouble *before* it gets out of hand. This is why it is important, at the outset, to research your market carefully, and check that there really is a demand for the type of service that you are offering.

You also need to have enough money to keep you going during the first months, while the business gets established. It is all too easy to under-estimate the initial costs, and it may take a while before you reach a level of sales which will comfortably cover your overheads. Start small, and watch every penny; you can expand once profits justify it.

Don't make the mistake of setting your prices too low. You may win extra trade in that way, but on the whole, price-cutting is not the best way to develop a business. It is better to aim for a high quality service, and to charge a fair price; customers are willing to pay, if the quality is right.

Do keep a close watch on your finances, and make sure that you can cover VAT and income tax demands as they fall due. Non-payment to the Inland Revenue and Customs & Excise is the cause of more bankruptcies than anything else.

Don't make the classic error of mistaking cash for profit. Just because your takings are high, it doesn't mean that you can go and blow all the money on a new car, a holiday or whatever. You need to work out your *profits*; and then allow for your own tax and National Insurance. The calculations can be quite sobering.

Lastly, one of the main problems: people. As we pointed out in Chapter 9, taking on a new member of staff is a major investment. You need to take considerable care with the interviewing and selection procedure, and then *develop* your staff with proper training. And both business partnerships, and employing members of your own family, are strong contenders for likely friction; do be careful in both these areas.

At the root of most business failure is bad management. Your hairdressing skills are very important, but you must also concentrate on running the business efficiently. This is why we strongly recommend that you take some form of small business training before you start up; research has shown that the chances of success are significantly improved for people who have taken such courses.

Looking to the future: planning for your retirement

Finally, a note on your pension. It may seem rather too soon to be thinking about retirement, if you are just starting up your own business, but in fact it is never too early to start planning. The tax advantages of contributing to a self-employed pension plan make it one of the best ways of saving for the future, because relief is given on your contributions at your top rate of tax on earned income. And if you don't bother to make provision, and rely totally on the state pension, you will experience a tremendous drop in your standard of living once you retire.

The beauty of some of the current plans on the market is that you do not even have to commit yourself to regular payments – if your income is irregular, or you are worried that a downturn in business could leave you unable to pay, you can contribute a series of lump sums – known as 'single premiums' – whenever you have extra cash to invest. The only constraint is that, to qualify for tax relief, you cannot invest more than 17.5 per cent of your net annual earnings (though you are allowed to 'average out' your contributions over any six-year period to arrive at an overall percentage per year of 17.5 per cent). Older people (born before 1933) can contribute an even higher percentage of their earnings.

There are all sorts of pension schemes and some of them are very heavily 'sold'. The best way of selecting a scheme suitable for your needs is to take advice from an independent insurance broker, specialising in pensions and life assurance.

Chapter 15
Further Information

Useful addresses

Wages Inspectorate
If you have any enquiries about minimum pay, holidays or holiday pay, contact the Senior Wages Inspector of the Department of Employment at one of the addresses below:

Fiveways House, Islington Row, Middleway, *Birmingham* B15 1SP; tel 021-643 8191
5th Floor, 125 Queens Road, *Brighton* BN1 3WB; tel 0273 23333
The Pithay, *Bristol* BS1 2NQ; tel 0272 273755
Pentland House, 47 Robb's Loan, *Edinburgh* EH14 1UE; tel 031-443 8731
BP House, *Hemel Hempstead*, Herts HP1 1DW; tel 0442 3714
City House, *Leeds* LS1 4JH; tel 0532 438232
Hanway House, Red Lion Square, *London* WC1R 4NH; tel 01-405 8454
Quay House, Quay Street, *Manchester* M3 3JE; tel 061-832 6506
Wellbar House, Gallowgate, *Newcastle upon Tyne* NE1 4TP; tel 0632 327575

ACAS (Advisory, Conciliation and Arbitration Service) regional offices
Advice on employment legislation is available from the regional offices at the following addresses:

Northern region: Westgate House, Westgate Road, Newcastle upon Tyne NE1 1TJ; tel 0632 612191
Yorkshire and Humberside region: Commerce House, St Alban's Place, Leeds LS2 8HH; tel 0532 431371

South East region: Clifton House, 83 Euston Road, London NW1 2RB; tel 01-388 5100
South West region: 16 Park Place, Clifton, Bristol BS8 1JP; tel 0272 211921
London region: Clifton House, 83 Euston Road, London NW1 2RB; tel 01-388 5100
Midlands region: Alpha Tower, Suffolk Street, Queensway, Birmingham B1 1TZ; tel 021-643 9911. Nottingham sub-office: 66 Houndsgate, Nottingham NG1 6BA; tel 0602 415450
North West region: Boulton House, 17 Chorlton Street, Manchester M1 3HY; tel 061-228 3222. Merseyside sub-office: Cressington House, 249 St Mary's Road, Garston, Liverpool L19 0NF: tel 051-427 8881
Scotland: Franborough House, 123 Bothwell Street, Glasgow G2 7JR; tel 041-204 2677
Wales: Phase 1, Ty Glas Road, Llanishen, Cardiff CF4 5PH; tel 0222 762636

Professional and trade associations
British Association of Professional Hairdressing Employers, (Managing agents for YTS),
   1 Barbon Close, Great Ormond Street, London WC1N 3JX; tel 01-405 7184
Caribbean and Afro Society of Hairdressers UK (CASH), PO Box 155, Bedford MK155 7SR
The Guild of Hairdressers, 24 Woodbridge Road, Guildford, Surrey GU1 1DY; tel 0483 67922
Hairdressing Council, 12 David House, 45 High Street, South Norwood, London SE25 6HJ; tel 01-771 6205
Hairdressing Manufacturers and Wholesalers Association, First Floor, Gillett House, 55 Basinghall Street, London EC2Y 5EA; tel 01-628 4321
Institute of Trichologists, 228 Stockwell Road, London SW9 9SU; tel 01-733 2056
National Hairdressers' Federation, 11 Goldington Road, Bedford MK40 3JY; tel 0234 60332

Beauty
British Association of Beauty Therapy and Cosmetology, Suite 5, Wolsely House, Oriel Road, Cheltenham, Glos GL50 1TH; tel 0242 570284 (also Confederation of International Beauty Therapy and Cosmetology)

British Association of Electrolysists, 16 Quakers Mede, Haddenham, Bucks HP17 8EB; tel 0844 290721
CIDESCO International Secretariat, PO Box 124, CH-8029 Zurich, Switzerland
International Health and Beauty Council, 109 Felpham Road, Felpham, West Sussex PO22 7PW
International Therapy Examination Council, 16 Avenue Place, Harrogate, North Yorkshire HG2 7PJ
Sun Tanning Advisory Bureau, 32 Grayshott Road, London SW11; tel 01-228 6077 (also Association of Sun Tanning Operators).

Other organisations mentioned in the book
British Franchise Association, Franchise Chambers, 75a Bell Street, Henley on Thames RG9 2BD; tel 0491 578049
Business in the Community ('Umbrella' organisation for Local Enterprise Agencies), 227A City Road, London EC1V 1LX; tel 01-235 3716; in Scotland: Scottish Business in the Community, Romano House, 43 Station Road, Corstorphine, Edinburgh EH12 7AF; tel 031-334 9876.
The Co-operative Development Agency, 21 Panton Street, London SW1Y 4DR; tel 01-839 2988
Hairdressing Training Board, Silver House, Silver Street, Doncaster DN1 1HL; tel 0302 342837
The Mechanical Copyright Society, Elgar House, 41 Streatham High Road, London SW16 1ER; tel 01-769 4400
Performing Rights Society Ltd, 29-33 Berners Street, London W1P 4AA; tel 01-580 5544
The Registrar of Companies for England and Wales, Companies Registration Office, Companies House, Crown Way, Maindy, Cardiff CF4 3UZ; tel 0222 388588
The Registrar of Companies for Scotland, Companies Registration Office, 102 George Street, Edinburgh EH2 3DJ; tel 031-225 5774

SHAC, 189a Old Brompton Road, London SW5 0AN; tel 01-373 7276/7841
The Small Landlords Association, 7 Rosedene Avenue, London SW16 2LS; tel 01-769 5060

Manufacturers and suppliers
This is a selected list, to get you started; a more comprehensive one is given in the annual *Hairdressers' Journal Trade Directory*.

Hair and beauty products
Clairol: Bristol-Myers (Clairol Salon Division), Station Road, Langley, Slough, Berks SL8 6EB; tel 75 44 266
Clynol: PO Box 4BW, Penn Road, Aylesbury, Bucks; tel 0296 28611
L'Oreal: 30 Kensington Church Street, London W8 4HA; tel 01-937 5454
Schwarzkopf: PO Box 4BW, Penn Road, Aylesbury, Bucks HP21 8HL; tel 0296 88101
Wella Great Britain: Wella Road, Basingstoke, Hants RG22 4AF; tel 0256 20202

Salon fittings and equipment
The Hairdressing and Beauty Equipment Centre, 262 Holloway Road, London N7 6NE; tel 01-607 7475
Ogee Ltd, Head Office: Kingston House, 240 Seaward Street, Glasgow G41 1NG; tel 041-429 7755
Pietranera (UK) Ltd, London Showroom: Emilia House, Mill Hill Industrial Estate, Flower Lane, Mill Hill, London NW7 2HU; tel 01-906 1911.
Distribution: Saxon Way, Melbourn, Nr Royston, Herts
Renbow International, Renbow House, Waterloo Terrace, London N1 1TF; tel 01-359 0917
Salon Services, Head Office: 150 Broomielaw, Glasgow G1; tel 041-248 5522
Wella Great Britain, Wella Road, Basingstoke, Hampshire RG22 4AF; tel 0256 20202

Training organisations
Alan International Schools, 54 Knightsbridge, London SW1X 7JN; tel 01-235 3131
International Salon Management, 36 Cyril Mansions, Prince of Wales Drive, London SW11 4HP; tel 01-622 7340
365 Hairdressing, Vine Tree House, Wendover, Bucks HP22 6EB; tel 0296 625454

For further reading

Hairdressers' Journal, published weekly by Business Press International Ltd, Quadrant House, The Quadrant, Sutton, Surrey SM2 5AS; tel 01-661 3500. Required reading – lots of useful tips on business, as well as the latest hair fashion scene.

Books

How you can make money in the hairdressing business, by Rosemary W Jeremiah (Stanley Thornes (Publishers) Ltd)
How to start and run your own business, by Gillian Clegg and Colin Barrow (Macmillan)
Management for hairdressers, by Carol Parsons (Macmillan)
Starting your own business, ed Edith Rudinger (Consumers' Association)
Working for yourself by Godfrey Golzen (Kogan Page)

There are also useful pamphlets available from government departments and Local Enterprise Agencies on all the aspects of running your own business.

Index

ACAS 63, 85, 133
Accidents 72, 116
Accountant 16, 37, 57-8, 65, 66
Accounts 23, 37, 65-6
Adult training 94
Advertising 25, 98, 100-102
   for staff 80-81
Advice, professional 57-63
Advisory, Conciliation and
   Arbitration Service, *see* ACAS
Air conditioning 51
Alan International 96, 134
Application form 82
Appointments book 23, 46, 114
Appraisal interview 88
Apprenticeship 92

Backwash 47, 48
Banks 36-8, 59, 66, 118
   loan 35
   manager 59, 124
   overdraft 35
Basins 47-8
Beautician 26, 96
Beauty:
   salon 124-8
   treatment chairs 48
Boiler 51, 117
Bookkeeping 57, 65-6, 123
Break-even point 34
British Franchise Association 18, 133
Budget 37
Building society 35, 36
Business:
   daily operation of 111-22
   interruption insurance 59
   names 29-31
   plan 36-7
   structure 14-17
   training 95-6

Business Expansion Scheme 36
Business in the Community 63, 133
Business transfer agents 20

Capital Radio Jobfinder 81
Careers office 81, 83
Cash:
   and carry 105
   book 65-6
   flow forecast 37
   handling 118
   on delivery 107
   petty 65
   register 118
Cashing up 118
Chairs 48
Checklist:
   for comparing properties 22
   of hairdressing equipment 52
   of printing requirements 99
   self-assessment 10
Cheques, returned 119
Christmas bonus 89
CIDESCO 96, 133
City & Guilds of London Institute
   92, 93
Cleaning 119-20
'Client Approach' 112
Client record cards 113
Cloakroom tickets 47
Clynol 96, 134
Coat cupboard 46
Colleges 83, 92
Colour theme 43
Commercial property agents 20
Communicating, with clients
   111-13
Company registration agents 16
Competitions 89, 103-4
Complaints 115-17

Computer 46, 56, 69, 113, 123
Confederation of International Beauty Therapy and Cosmetology 96, 133
Contract of employment 73, 84
Converting a shop 24-6
Co-operative 17
Costs:
   controlling 120
   of starting the business 32-3
   running 33-4
Credit:
   reference 107
   terms 107
Crises 10, 117-18
Customs & Excise 57, 66, 129

Dalton's Weekly 20
Decorating 41-3
Directors (of limited companies) 16, 67, 68
Discounts 103
Discrimination 77
Dismissal 75-6, 85
Dispensary 53-4
Display area 46
Dressing-out tables 47

Ear piercing 125
Electrical wiring 25, 43, 122
Employers' liability insurance 59, 76-7
Employing staff 73-7
Employment agencies 83
Enterprise Agencies 63
Enterprise Allowance Scheme 39
Entertainment 114-15
Entrance (of salon) 55
Equipment 47-56
Estate agents 20
Expansion 123
Eyelash and eyebrow tinting 125

Fidelity guarantee insurance 60
Filing system 113
Finance houses 39
Finding a salon 20-22
Fire:
   certificate 122
   precautions 72, 122
First aid 72, 122
First year operators 92
Fixtures and fittings 24, 25, 47-56

Flat (over shop) 28
Floor coverings 51-2
Food 115
Forecasting 69
Franchising 14, 17, 18
Freehold 27
Freelance hairdressers 77
Frozen water pipes 117

Going concern 21-4
Goodwill 24
Gowns 53, 119
Guild of Hairdressers 62, 132

Hairdressers' Journal 15, 20, 80, 110, 125, 134
Hairdressing Council 62, 92, 93, 132
Hairdressing schools 93
Hairdressing Training Board 92, 93, 133
Hairdryers 49
Health and Safety at Work Act 1974 71-2
Health insurance 60, 89
Heating 51
Hire purchase 32, 43
Hot water system 51, 117
Hours of opening 72
Humidifiers 53

Incentives 8, 89
Income tax 14, 65, 67-8, 129
Inland Revenue 57, 60, 65, 68, 87, 129
Insurance 35, 58, 59-61, 90
Interest payments 35
International Health and Beauty Council 96, 133
International Salon Management 96, 134
International Therapy Examination Council 96, 133
Interviews 83-4
   appraisal 88
Ionisers 53
Itemised pay statement 73, 87

Jobcentre 79, 80, 81
Job Training Scheme 94

Keyman insurance 60

Laundry 53, 119
Law 70-78

Index

Layout 41
Lease 27, 58, 71
Leasing (equipment) 32, 43
Legal:
  expenses insurance 60
  requirements 70-78
Letting 28
Life insurance 35
Lighting 50-51
Limited company 16, 57
Loan 35-6, 38
Local authority 39, 63, 70, 71
Local Enterprise Agencies 63
Location 19-20
Logo 54, 98, 99
L'Oreal 96, 104, 134
Loss, of clients' property 116

Make-up service 125
Manager, employing 8, 124
Manicure 126
Manufacturers 106, 133-4
Marketing 97-104
Market research 19-20, 27-8, 97
Maternity pay 75
Mechanical Copyright Society 56, 133
Mirrors 49
Model nights 95
Mortgage 35, 36
Music 55-6, 114

Names 29-31
National Hairdressers' Federation 61-2, 85, 92, 132
National Insurance 16, 34, 60, 68-9, 74
Negligence 78
New technology 56
New unit 26

Offices, Shops and Railway Premises Act 1963 71
Ogee 43, 134
Overdraft 35, 38
Overheads 33-4
Overhead equipment 47
Overtime 74
Own-brand packaging 107

Partnership 9, 15-16
PAYE 14, 16, 34, 67, 68, 74, 87
Pay, Christmas bonus 89
  holiday pay 74
  itemised statement of 73, 87
  maternity pay 75
  sick pay 74
  weekly or monthly 87
Payment (of suppliers) 107
Pension contributions 60, 129-30
Performing Rights Society 56, 133
Permanent health insurance 60
Petty cash 65
Phonographic Performance Ltd 115
Photographs 50, 104
Pilfering 120-21
Pipes, frozen 117
Planning permission 22, 24, 58, 70
Plants 53
Plumbing 25, 41, 43
Premises 19-29
Premium 32
Price-list 46
Pricing 32, 34-5, 64-5, 129
Private hairdressing schools 93
Private limited company 16
Private loan 35-6
Professional advice 57-63
Profit-sharing 8, 17, 89
Pro-forma payment 107
Promotions 100-104
Public liability insurance 59, 78
Public relations 102-103

Radio 55-6, 101
Raising capital 32-40, 57, 59
Reception 43, 46-7
Receptionist 46
Record cards 113
Redundancy 76
Refresher courses 93
Refreshments 53, 114
Rent a chair 26, 77, 90
Representatives 106
Research 19-20, 27-8, 97
Restrictive covenants 22, 24
Retailing 128
Retirement 129
Returned cheques 119
Running costs 33-4

Safes 118
Safety 71-2, 122
Sale of Goods Act 78

139

Sales:
   display 46, 112
   representatives 106
Salon:
   decor 43
   entertainment 114-15
   fittings 41, 43
   image 97
   layout 41
   maintenance 120
   manager 124
   second 124
   security 46, 120-21
   training 94-5
Salon Services 43, 134
Schwarzkopf 104, 134
Scottish Business in the Community 63
Screens 55
Security:
   for business loan 10, 16, 38
   in salon 46, 120
Selling 97-104
Seven Point Plan 79-80
Shop:
   front 54-5
   hours 72
   sign 54, 97
Shrinkage 120-21
Sick pay 74
Small Firms Service 63
Sole trader 14-15, 57, 67
Solicitor 58-9, 70, 85
Special offers 103
Staff 73-7, 79-90
   appearance of 98
   meetings 87-8
   shortage 117-18
   supervision 49
State Registered Hairdresser 62
Stationery 33, 99-100
Stealing 120-21
Stock 24, 33, 52, 53-4, 105-10, 120
   control 107-109
   room 53-4
   rotation 107-9
   taking 109

Styling units 47, 112
Sunbeds 127-8
Suppliers 105-6, 134
Supply of Goods and Services Act 1982 78

Taped music 56
Tax, *see* income tax, PAYE, VAT
Term assurance 60
Term loan 38
Theft 120-21
365 Hairdressing 96, 135
'Through the Looking Glass' 11, 89, 104, 113
Till 46, 65, 118
Tips 87
Toilets 54
Towels 48, 119
Trade associations 61-2, 132-3
Trade Descriptions Acts 78
Trade Fairs 41, 56, 109
Trading legislation 78
Training 56, 62, 89, 91-6
Trichology 128

Unfair dismissal 75-6

Wages:
   book 65, 66
   Council 7, 74, 86
   Inspectorate 131
Wall photographs 50
Waiting area 46
Wall-mounted equipment 47
Washing machine 53
Washroom 54
Water system 51, 117
Wella 96, 104, 112, 134
Wholesalers 105
Windows 55, 97
Working capital 33
Working positions 41, 47

VAT 14, 16, 57, 65, 66-7, 90, 129
Video 46, 56, 115
Viewing property 21-2

YTS 93-4